the | Names of God

A Series of Sermons about what God says about Himself.

By

Dr Ellis F. André

(Sermons delivered in 2012)

FOREWORD

My dad wrote prolifically, mostly sermons and lecture notes. From my earliest memories, books, notepads, pens, highlighters, and in subsequent years, his laptop, were always close at hand. He was both a student and a teacher. He probably had a good many books in him, however these never materialised into published works.

Following a number of requests for a particularly popular sermon series on the names of God, my mom, Ruth, decided that she would collate all the sermon manuscripts and is pleased to have the opportunity to publish these. These sermons were initially preached when he pastored at Rosebank Union Church, in South Africa, and were further developed and preached with an accompanying personal / small group study guide, in 2012 at White Rock Baptist Church, in Canada.

My dad was an inspiring preacher and teacher with a love for God and His Word. He was grounded in reality, had a great sense of humour and was loved and appreciated by his congregations and students. As the eternal student himself, I know that my dad knew and experienced God in a deeper and more personal way, as a result of grappling with God's revelation of Himself. He loved to share his learnings with others.

The manuscripts are the essence of the sermons as they were delivered. As he interacted with those in the congregation, and as he felt prompted by the Holy Spirit, he would improvise, adding a comment, a nuance, sharing a story, illustrating a fact, adapting a conclusion, as he felt moved to do so. While these nuances aren't captured in the manuscripts, I nonetheless found the reading of these sermons causing me to be more in awe of God, more grateful for His love and more enthusiastic in my service of Him.

So, whatever your knowledge or understanding of God, if you'd like to know more about how God's character is revealed through the names by which He was known and how this revelation allows us to know Him more intimately ... then this series of sermons is for you! May you experience God and trust Him completely!

Rozanne Hammer

Cape Town, South Africa, June 2021

Contents

What's in a Name? 3

Yahweh: God's "Proper" Name 13

Adonai: Gracious Lord and Master 24

El Elyon: God Most High 35

El Ro'i: The God Who Sees Me 46

"*El Shaddai:* The All-Sufficient God" 55

El Olam: the Everlasting God 65

Yahweh Yireh: The LORD will Provide 75

Yahweh Nissi: The LORD my Banner 83

Yahweh Rophecha: The LORD Who Heals You 93

Yahweh Shalom: The LORD our Peace 102

Yahweh Ts'vaot: The LORD Almighty 115

Yahweh Ro'i: The LORD is my Shepherd 126

Yahweh Tsidqenu: The LORD our Righteousness 137

Yahweh Meqaddishchem: The LORD Who Makes You Holy 143

Yahweh Shammah: The LORD is There 153

INTRODUCTION

In revealing himself as Elohim, Yahweh, and Adonai, God gives us insight into his might, his self-existence, his attachment to and love for his creation, his faithfulness, and his benevolent sovereignty.

How magnificently great God is! We can trust him completely (The one and only God is Elohim, he is Yahweh and he is Adonai: our response to him as Elohim, the all-powerful God, is wonder and awe; our response to him as Yahweh, the gracious God of the covenant, is love and gratitude; our response to him as Adonai, the sovereign Lord and Master, is submission and service).

Conceptual Purpose
To introduce the hearers to the idea that names are important in the Scriptures and that the names by which God has made himself known to us are particularly important in that they reveal his character to us.

Affective Purpose
To inspire a sense of confidence in the hearers as they begin to see something of the manifold greatness of God

Behavioural Purpose
To influence the hearers to trust God more fully in view of the attributes revealed in the names Elohim, Yahweh, and Adonai.

Visionary Purpose
To raise the level of expectation in the church regarding what God is able to do so that we do not constantly cut him down to our size.

What's in a Name?

Readings: Genesis 1:1-3; Exodus 3:13-15; Psalm 8

WE COMMENCE A NEW SERIES THIS MORNING, A SERIES THAT HAS THE POTENTIAL TO TRANSFORM US AS INDIVIDUALS AND AS A CHURCH.

You may have heard the lyrics of some songs that incorporate Hebrew names for God and wondered what the precise significance of these names is. Songs like:

Jehovah Jireh, my Provider

El Shaddai

The words of El Shaddai incorporate three of the divine names:
    El Shaddai, El Shaddai,
    El-Elyon na Adonai,
    Age to age You're still the same,
    By the power of the name.
    El Shaddai, El Shaddai,
    Erkamka na Adonai,
    We will praise and lift You high,
    El Shaddai.

I have some good news for you this morning.

This is not rocket science and you don't have to know Hebrew. If we are serious, we will come to understand God better and we will get to know him more intimately. In his classic, *Knowing God*, J. I. Packer stated simply, "A little knowledge *of* God is worth more than a great deal of knowledge *about* him."[1]

There will be an experiential and devotional emphasis in this series. As we learn key truths about God, we will ask, "So what? What does this mean when I feel totally isolated and alone, or if I receive some really distressing news? What implications does this have for my business dealings? What does this mean when I am going through a really rough patch? And how will it help me to pray?

This morning I am going to lay some of the groundwork necessary if we are to derive benefit from this study.

WHAT'S IN A NAME? (NAMES IN GENERAL)

When we ask, "What's in a name?" we are implying that the words we use to describe people are not, in themselves, that important. In one sense, we are right. The adage itself comes from one of Shakespeare's plays. It was Juliet, who said to Romeo:

> What's in a name?
> That which we call a rose
> by any other name
> would smell as sweet.

We tend to regard names as labels, sounds associated with people, rather than as single-word descriptions of the person, summing up their character. But an adage such as this could never have arisen in Israel. To the Israelites names were of real consequence. They virtually represented the person to whom they belonged. A name conveyed something that was distinctive about its bearer. A person

---

[1] J. I. Packer, Knowing God (London: Hodder and Stoughton, 1975), 22 (emphasis added).

was virtually indistinguishable from their name. Many statements in Scripture only make sense when we understand that there was a definite relationship between a name and its bearer (Psa 7:17; 113:1-3; Prov 18:12; Ezra 6:12; Acts 4:12).

That is why our attention is drawn to the meaning of names in the Bible.

How would you like to have been named *Maher-shalal-hash-baz* -- "Quick to the plunder swift to the spoil?" That's what the prophet Isaiah named his son (Isa 8:1-4). And there was a very good reason for it. I think they must have called him Basil for short.

Then there was a man called Nabal. He was a crass and surly so-and-so who so antagonised David that David was ready to take him out. But Nabal's beautiful and intelligent wife, Abigail, interceded for her idiot of a husband, pleading with David to spare his life. Listen to her entreaty: "Please, my lord, pay no attention to this wicked man, Nabal. He is just like his name—his name is 'Fool' and folly goes with him" (1 Sam 25:25).

Why do you think God sometimes changed a person's name? For example, Abram's name was changed to Abraham ("Father of many"). When Rachael was giving birth to Joseph's baby brother, she was in extreme anguish and actually died in childbirth. She wanted to call the baby Ben-oni - "Son of my sorrow," but Jacob would have none of it and he called his newborn son Benjamin - "Son of my right hand" (Gen 35:16-18). We could go on and on. Simon was given the name Peter (a "rock"). Nowhere is the significance of names more evident that when an angel instructed Joseph to call his stepson "*Jesus* . . . because he will save his people from their sins" (Matt 1:21). *Jeshua* (Jesus' Hebrew name) means "salvation."

There's more to this subject than we may have imagined, but does it really matter to us in the 21st century? Absolutely!

SUPPOSE THAT GOD HAD SOME SPECIFIC THINGS TO SAY TO US ABOUT *HIMSELF*.

And suppose that he actually revealed himself to us by giving us a series of related but distinct names and compound names. Suppose further that he unfolded these names at defining moments in his interaction with his people and that they represent important insights into his character. Suppose that it is really not difficult for us English-speakers to identify these names and that they enlarge our vision of God. Suppose also that an awareness of these names enlarge our vision of God and their meanings help to us in our walk with the Lord and particularly in our prayer lives.

This is precisely what happens in the Hebrew Scriptures. And, with a little help, we can know what these names are and what they mean. Some of us can probably remember when most movies were in black and white and how enthusiastically people greeted the advent of movies in technicolor. What a difference that made. Nowadays 3D and Imax movies add a new dimension. Contrast between an old TV and watching in High Definition. In a sense, a basic awareness of the names of God can add a dimension to our reading a Scripture. More importantly, it will help us to know God better.

So let's lay the groundwork. Please take your Bible and turn to the very first chapter of Genesis (Gen. 1:1-3).

THERE ARE THREE FOUNDATIONAL NAMES OR TITLES WITH WHICH WE MUST ACQUAINT OURSELVES.

Elohim

God is the subject of the very first sentence in the Bible. The word translated God is *Elohim*. It occurs no fewer than 32 times in Genesis 1 alone and over 2 550 times in the Hebrew Scriptures. There are three important things I need to say about this name.

It is more than a generic name for deity. When Elohim is used to refer to God, it is used very much as a personal name. So, for example, we hear David pray to Elohim: "O God, you are my God, earnestly I seek you; my soul thirsts for you" (Psa 63:1). This should not surprise us because there is only one true God and he is a personal God.

The word *Elohim* is believed to be derived from a Hebrew root meaning "strength" or "might." The main idea conveyed by the name is that of absolute power. It is God who calls the universe into being by the power of his word. Absolutely everything has its origin in him and he is sovereign over all that exists.

We see him in Genesis 1 calling this vast universe into being. We hear him speak. By the power of his almighty word, he decrees. We read: "And *Elohim* said . . . and it was so!" (Gen. 1:9, 11 etc.) "By the word of the LORD were the heavens made, their starry host by the breath of his mouth (Psa 33:6).

Elohim is a plural word but it is used with singular verbs. The suffix "im" is much like our "s" in English. So, Genesis 1:1 reads literally: "In the beginning Gods he created the heavens and the earth." It is a mistake (an anachronism) to liken this to the so-called "royal we" or the plural of majesty.

Some have suggested that the use of the plural here draws attention to the inexhaustible fullness in God. It certainly does! Others have inferred that this plural anticipates the doctrine of the Trinity. It would be wrong to assert that the first verse in the Bible actually *teaches* that God is triune. But the word certainly *allows* for the richness subsequently revealed as God unfolds his trinitarian nature. In fact, these two ideas are complementary: the richness of God's trinitarian life is an important dimension of God's fullness.

Yahweh

We don't go very far before we encounter another name for God. In Genesis 2:4, we read: "When the LORD God created the heavens and the earth. . . ." Here's an important piece of information. Whenever you see the word LORD (all upper case letters) in the Old Testament it is a rendering of the name Yahweh. In Genesis 2, it is purposely combined with Elohim, but usually we encounter the name on its own. The name *Yahweh* occurs no fewer than 6 828 times in Scripture. While other designations of God are used as names, strictly-speaking Yahweh is the personal or proper name by which God has chosen to make himself known (Ex 3:13-15; 6:2-5; 34:4-7).

We are going to focus on this name next week but I do need to make a few comments in the context of this morning's message.

Yahweh is God's "covenant name." If in the name Elohim the emphasis is on God's might, in the name Yahweh the emphasis is on his faithfulness. He is the God who enters into relationship with his people. He is the God who comes looking for Adam and Eve. He is the God who makes them a garment of animal skins. He is the God who never stops seeking us no matter how far we go.

You may wonder why we are using the name *Yahweh* and not *Jehovah*. There were no written vowels in Hebrew. Vowel points (the dots and dashes we see under Hebrew letters) were introduced when Hebrew was no longer a (widely) spoken language. God's name is represented by four consonants, transliterated YHWH, but the Jews felt it was too holy to pronounce. When they read aloud they substituted the word *Adonai* (Lord). Centuries later, when vowel points were introduced into the consonantal text, the vowels of the word *Adonai* were inserted into the Tetragrammaton (YHWH; JHVH in German). This gives us "Jahovah" (and subsequently *Jehovah*). It doesn't matter all that much; it is not the vocalization of the name that is important but its meaning.

Suffice it to say this morning that the main thoughts conveyed by the name *Yahweh* is that he is always present and completely faithful. He is the God who does not write off his creation. He enters into a covenant relationship with his people.

Adonai

We sometimes come across the word Lord spelt a little differently. When we read LORD (all upper case letters), it is a rendering of Yahweh, but we also encounter the word Lord (spelled Capital "L" and lower case "ord"). In such cases it translates the word *Adonai*.

If we look at Psalm 8, for example, we read, "O LORD (Yahweh), our Lord (Adonai), how majestic is your name in all the earth."

In Isaiah 6 the prophet tells us, "In the year that King Uzziah died, I saw the Lord (Adonai) seated on a throne. . . ." Isaiah feared for his life because he had seen the LORD Almighty (Yahweh Tsava'ōth). Then he heard the voice of the Lord (Adonai) saying, "Whom shall I send? And who will go for us?"

The word *Adonai* can be used as a general designation for a superior. In Modern Hebrew, "Adoni" means "Sir." "Adon" can even mean "Mr."

But when the word refers to God in Scripture it is always in the plural and it portrays him as the rightful Lord over all creation. He is a gracious and benevolent Master. We shall look at this title more thoroughly in a few weeks.

BUT EVEN AT THIS EARLY STAGE WE CAN MAKE SOME SIGNIFICANT STATEMENTS ABOUT THESE THREE FOUNDATIONAL NAMES OF GOD.

When we invoke God as **Elohim**, we are thinking primarily of his might and his majesty. When we call upon him as **Yahweh** the focus is on his active presence and his faithfulness. He is the God who says, "I myself will be there; you can count on me." "I am who I have always been." When we honour him as **Adonai**, we recognize him not only as the rightful sovereign over all creation but also as our gracious Lord and Master.

But this is not an exercise in abstract theology. God unveils his names to us not in the ivory tower of speculation but in the midst (hustle and bustle) of life.

1. Let say you receive some distressing news. It could be the betrayal of a friend. Or it could be an unfavourable diagnosis when you went to see the doctor. It could be when your needs are great you lose your job. How do you react to any one of these circumstances? Will God still be with you? Is he still Elohim? Has his word lost its ancient power? Can he who called the universe into being not intervene in your circumstance? Is he still Yahweh? Will he be actively present with you in your crisis? Can you count

on his faithfulness? Is he still Adonai your Lord? Can you look to him as a slave would look to his or her faithful master? Is he still a compassionate master, Adonai?
2. Suppose the Church was presented with a significant ministry opportunity and it is way beyond the natural capacity of the people? After prayer the people in spite of it seemingly being farfetched, that this is what God wants. This is who God is. Why should he call us to do things that are within our limited ability? If he is God and we are trusting him, do we bring Elohim into the picture? He never commands without him providing the ability or the where-with-all to do it. We either factor him in or we factor him out.
3. Perhaps you are standing on the brink of a new challenge in your life. It might be exciting but also daunting. But God is Elohim; God is Yahweh; God is Adonai. He is all-powerful. He is faithful. He is Lord. He says to you, "I will be with you."

So, the one God is Elohim, he is Yahweh, and he is Adonai. Our response to him as *Elohim*, the all-powerful God, is wonder and awe. Our response to him as *Yahweh*, the gracious God of the covenant, is love and gratitude. And our response to him as *Adonai*, the Sovereign Lord and Master, is submission and service. He is still our compassionate Master.

Conclusion
Do you want to stay exactly where you are in your walk with the Lord or do you want to know God better than you do? He wants to reveal himself to you. May the LORD himself create in us a genuine hunger to know him better.

Please join me on a journey as we seek to know God better. We shall learn many things about him. But, more importantly, we shall have the opportunity to come to know him more intimately. J. I. Packer spoke volumes when he said, "A little knowledge *of* God is worth more than a great deal of knowledge *about* him."

Do you sincerely want to know God better?

As you open your heart to God, he will open his great heart to you.

יְהוָה

Yahweh: God's "Proper" Name

Readings: Exodus 3:1-15 (34:4-7; Psalm 103:1-22; Isaiah 43:10-13)

This morning we are considering the name *Yahweh*. This is the second in a series on the names by which God has revealed himself to us in Scripture. Before we get into it, I need to refer briefly to three important building blocks which I tried to set in place last week:

- Names are extremely important in Scripture. We tend to use names as labels, sounds associated with people, but in the Bible a name conveys something very important about the person to whom it belongs.

- God has identified himself by giving us a number of related names and compound names.

- With relatively little effort, we can understand what these names mean and why they are used. This helps us to read the Bible in high definition. And this is not take-it-or-leave-it theoretical knowledge. I can assure you that an appreciation of the names of God will help you in your spiritual life.

This morning we are looking at what some have called God's "proper" name, *Yahweh*.

GOD'S REVELATION AT THE FOOT OF THE MOUNT SINAI (THE BURNING BUSH).

Moses' State of Mind

Come with me this morning to a dry and arid region. An eighty-year-old man is tending the flock of his father-in-law. He is remarkably fit and in good shape, physically that is. He is getting on with life. In fact, he's been doing that for forty long years. He has quite a story to tell, but he doesn't talk much about himself.

The Abortive Attempt

Truth is sometimes stranger than fiction. And, to put it mildly, this man's story is incredible. Destined for death as a Hebrew baby in Egypt, he had been found and adopted by Pharaoh's daughter. He had lived as a prince in Egypt. But, as the writer to the Hebrews tells us, "By faith Moses, when he had grown up, refused to be known as the son of Pharaoh's daughter. He chose to be mistreated along with the people of God rather than to enjoy the pleasures of sin for a short time" (Heb 11:24-25). He had no doubt come to realise that it was no accident that he, a Hebrew, found himself in the household of the king of Egypt. But he did the right thing at the wrong time and in the wrong way altogether. He saw a cruel Egyptian beating a Hebrew slave, intervened and killed the man. The next day, he tried to settle a fight between two of the Hebrew slaves. The aggressor rejected his intervention with a terse remark: "Who made you ruler and judge over us?" (Ex 2:14). Moses had incurred Pharaoh's wrath and had to flee from Egypt. As Stephen tells us, "Moses thought that his own people would realize that God was using him to rescue them, but they did not" (Acts 7:25).

Dashed Dreams and Resignation

Scripture is silent regarding Moses' psychological state during those forty long years, but we can only imagine: dashed dreams, disillusionment and resignation. Perhaps he had misread the signs. If God had a plan for Moses' life, Moses himself had well and truly kiboshed it. Tending your father-in-law's flock in the Sinai desert is not a stimulating life for one of the best educated men alive. Life is uneventful, but at least it's safe in that desolate part of the world.

Another day awaits Moses; another uneventful day as he leads Jethro's flock to the far side of the desert.

The Revelation at the Burning Bush
In the distance he notices that an acacia bush had caught alight and is burning in the scorching heat of the Sinai desert. He's seen that before and he knows that the dry shrub will soon burn out. They always do. But this bush just keeps on burning. So he decides to go over and see the strange sight for himself.

As he approaches the burning bush, he hears a voice from within:

"Moses, Moses," He responds, "Here I am."
"Do not come any closer. Take off your sandals, for the place where you are standing is holy ground." Then he said, "I am the God of your father, the God of Abraham, the God of Isaac, and the God of Jacob." At this Moses hid his face, because he was afraid to look at God.
The LORD said 'I have indeed seen the misery of my people in Egypt. I have heard them crying out because of their slave drivers, and I am concerned about their suffering. So I have come down to rescue them from the hand of the Egyptians and to bring them up out of the land into a good and spacious land, a land flowing with milk and honey. . . . So now, go, I am sending you to Pharaoh to bring my people the Israelites out of Egypt." (Ex. 3:4-10)

Moses raised no fewer than five objections. It is the second one that is of particular relevance to us this morning.

"What is His Name?"
"Suppose I go to the Israelites and say to them, 'The God of your fathers has sent me to you,' and they ask me, 'What is his name?' Then what shall I tell them?"

The ensuing interchange is extremely important so let's look at it closely. God says to Moses, "I AM WHO I AM." This is what you are to say to the Israelites: 'I AM has sent me to you.'"

God also said to Moses, "Say to the Israelites, 'Yahweh, the God of your fathers—the God of Abraham, the God of Isaac, and the God of Jacob—has sent me to you.' This is my name forever, the name by which I am to be remembered from generation to generation."

To some God's response to Moses may even sound as if God was telling Moses to mind his own business. In other words, he was saying, 'Moses, I don't have to tell you what my name is. I am who I am." But nothing could be further from the truth. God is about to *reveal* his name, not to *conceal* it.

In fact there is an intentional relationship between the Hebrew word for "I AM" and the name *Yahweh*. The word "I AM" is *ehyeh* and the name *Yahweh* is believed to be derived from the same root. "I am who I am" certainly underlines the fact that God is the source of his own life. Everyone and everything else had a beginning and owes their existence to another. Not God! In Revelation he is described as the one "who is and who was and who is to come" (Rev 1:8). He is eternal.

But there is more to this. It is not a metaphysical statement about God's eternal existence. It underlines his presence and his faithfulness. Some suggest that God is saying something like "I am who I have always been." It has to do with God's *presence*. Old

Testament scholar, Theodor Vriezen, expressed the thought conveyed by the name in the statement, "I myself will be there; count on me."[2]

Yahweh is the one who is actively present. He is not remote or aloof. Whether we know it or not, he is always near and he intervenes on behalf of his people. He says to Moses and he says to us, "I have indeed *seen*, I have *heard*, and *I am concerned* about your situation."

Your situation may be very different from that of the Israelites in Egyptian bondage, but you may well wonder whether God is as real today as he was in times past. The Israelites had reason to wonder. In one sense, it must have helped to hear stories about God's faithfulness to Abraham, Isaac, and Jacob. In another, it might have exacerbated their situation. If those stories were true, why is their situation so dismal? Has God changed? Does he care? You may not doubt the affirmations we Christians make about God's essential nature, but you may wonder about his apparent absence? Where is he in your moment of crisis? Contained within the very name of God is some highly relevant and wonderful news.

From the time of this revelation to Moses, the name *Yahweh* became the primary name for God. The name itself speaks volumes. There are over 6 800 references to the name in the Old Testament, so it is not difficult to form a picture of who *Yahweh* is and what his name means. All we have to do is read every one of the references and then draw our conclusions. Fortunately, we can come to some

---

[2] Th. C. Vriezen, An Outline of Old Testament Theology, 2nd ed. (Wageningen, The Netherlands: H. Veenman and Zonen nv, 1970), 180. The Hebrew verb "to be" does not convey the abstract notion of being implied in the Greek and modern contexts. "On the contrary God is in Israel the one who is always really present" (Ibid., 181).

accurate conclusions without having to read every single verse in which his name is mentioned.

But before we draw some important conclusions, there is another passage that helps to fill out the picture. It also involves Moses.

GOD'S REVELATION ON THE SUMMIT OF MOUNT SINAI

Yahweh's Gracious Hand

We move on several months. Behind us are a series of unprecedented events. Nothing like this had ever happened before and nothing like it has ever happen subsequently. Since the appearance of God to Moses at the burning bush, he has seen the most extraordinary events. The Israelites can have no reasonable doubt that *Yahweh* is God—the one and only God. He has opened a way through the Sea of Reeds. He has provided water and food for them. He has manifested his presence in a dramatic and awe-inspiring manner at Sinai. He is certainly "living up to his Name." In fact, they are beginning to understand what the Name means.

Idolatry at the Foot of Mount Sinai

But, despite all of this, the people lapse into idolatry right in the shadow of Mount Sinai. Before they even leave the mountain, they breach the covenant in the most flagrant and sordid way. Incredible!

Clearly Moses is disgusted with his brother Aaron and the people. God says to Moses, "Let me destroy them. Then I will make you into a great nation" (Ex 32:9-10). But Moses intercedes for the people. His audience with the LORD is telling and so poignant. Before Jesus, no one ever got closer to God than Moses. God tells him that the people are so stiff-necked that he will send an angel with them, but that his Presence cannot accompany them lest they incur his judgment.

God's Presence
But Moses pleads with him: "If your presence does not go up with us, do not send us up from here" (Ex 33:15). We haven't got a hope.

Moses knew for a fact what we have to keep learning. If we imagine that we can accomplish anything of spiritual value without him, we are sadly mistaken. God is holy and Moses knows that this in itself constitutes a danger, but he realises that we dare not move without him.

He realises that it is every bit as difficult to lead the people through the desert as it was to get them out of Egypt. So he asks, "*Show me your glory*." He was not looking for a spiritual high, some kind of blessing for its own sake. He can imagine what lies ahead. He knows that both he and the people will need God's grace and presence daily if they are to make it to the Promised Land.

In response to this bold request the LORD says, "I will cause all my goodness to pass in front of you, and I will proclaim my name Yahweh in your presence. I will have mercy on whom I will have mercy, and I will have compassion on whom I will have compassion." But he said, "You cannot see my face for no one can see me and live. . . . There is a place near me where you may stand on a rock. When my glory passes by, I will put you in a cleft in the rock, and cover you with my hand until I have passed by. Then I will remove my hand and you will see my back; but my face must not be seen" (Ex 33:19-23).

God's Glory and the Name
God told Moses to present himself on the top of Mount Sinai on the next morning. "Then the LORD came down in the cloud and stood there with him and proclaimed his name, Yahweh. And he passed in front of Moses, proclaiming, 'Yahweh, Yahweh, the compassionate and gracious God, slow to anger, abounding in love and faithfulness,

maintaining love to thousands, and forgiving wickedness, rebellion, and sin. Yet he does not leave the guilty unpunished. . .'" (Ex 34:5-7).

"When Moses came down from Mount Sinai . . . he was not aware that his face was radiant because he had spoken with *Yahweh*" (Ex 34:29). Moses' brother, Aaron, and the Israelites were afraid to come near him.

This is as close as we get to a biblical definition of the name *Yahweh* (though no definition could ever do him justice). Terms like compassionate, gracious, abounding in love and faithfulness. All this without forfeiting his righteousness!

So much could be said about this but I can do no better than to focus on a word that occurs twice in this passage and hundreds of times in the Old Testament. It is the Hebrew word *chesed* and it is translated in a number of ways: love, everlasting kindness; unfailing love, mercy, steadfast love (see 2 Sam 7:15; Psa 103:17; Psa 136:1-2; Isa 54:8, 10). It is virtually the Old Testament equivalent of the word *agapē* in the New Testament. It involves a combination of deep feeling with unswerving faithfulness. Earlier in the service, we read from Psalm 103. In a few verses we encounter that word twice: "As high as the heavens are above the earth, so great is his *chesed* for those who fear him. . . . From everlasting to everlasting, Yahweh's *chesed* is with those who fear him (Psa 103:14, 17).

LET ME TRY TO PUT THIS IN A NUTSHELL

There are four key ideas associated with the Name that I need to emphasize.

In the first place, we know that **Yahweh is unique**. When Moses conveys the message to Pharaoh, "This is what Yahweh, the God of

Israel, says, 'Let my people go . . . ,'" Pharaoh retorts, "Who is Yahweh that I should obey him and let Israel go? I do not know Yahweh and I will not let Israel go" (Ex 5:1-2). Well, in due course, Pharaoh found out! As God says through the prophet Isaiah, ""Before me no god was formed, nor will there be one after me. I, even I, am *Yahweh*, and apart from me there is no saviour" (Isa 43:11-12). He is the one and only God!

Second, **for *Yahweh* nothing is more important than relationship**. When we use the name *Yahweh,* we are focusing on God as the God who has an ongoing relationship with his people. He does not *need* us. But, out of the overflow of his love, he creates us so that we can enjoy a relationship with him. He walks with Adam in the cool of the day. He comes looking for Adam and Eve when they sin. He calls Abram and establishes a covenant with him.

As we read through the Old Testament, we are amazed at the lengths to which he will go. Israel repeatedly breaks the terms of the covenant and has to go into captivity. God compares her to a wife who keeps committing adultery. He should get rid of her. But he says, "How can I give you up Israel? How can I hand you over, Israel? My heart is changed within me. All my compassion is aroused" (Hos 11:8).

But it is when we see Jesus that we understand the lengths to which *Yahweh* will go to re-establish a relationship with you and me. "In Christ God was reconciling the world to himself" (2 Cor 5:19). The angel announces that the name of Mary's son will be Jesus because he will save his people from their sin. (*Yeshua* is a contraction of *Yehoshua* which means "Yahweh saves" (Matt 1:21)[3]

---

[3] In Romans 10:9-13, Paul refers to Jesus as the Lord and applies a verse in Joel to him. There can be no doubt that he is referring to Jesus when he says, "Everyone who calls on the name of the Lord (Greek: Kurios) will be saved" (Rom 10:13). In

Remember, he doesn't need us. As *Yahweh*, he is complete in himself. But, as *Yahweh*, he is faithful to his word and he loves us in spite of ourselves. As amazing as it may seem, *Yahweh* is the God who wants nothing more than to have a relationship with you.

Third, **Yahweh is the God who is actively present with his people.** As we noted, "I AM WHO I AM" is not an abstract statement about existence. It conveys the sense: "I myself will be there; count on me." And he cares!

Fourth, **Yahweh is the God who is absolutely faithful to his covenant.**

We could refer to passage after passage to illustrate the faithfulness of *Yahweh*, but here are two that express God's commitment in no uncertain terms, one from the Old and the other from the New Testament.

> But Zion said, "*Yahweh* has forsaken me,
> my Lord has forgotten me."
> "Can a mother forget the baby at her breast
> and have no compassion on the child she has borne?
> Though she may forget,
> I will not forget you!
> See, I have engraved you on the palms of my hands;
> Your walls are ever before me (Isa 49:14-16).
>
> What then shall we say in response to this? If God is for us, who can be against us? He who did not spare his own Son, but gave him up for us all—how will he not also, along with him,

---

Joel, the verse reads, "And everyone who calls on the name of the LORD (Yahweh) will be saved" (Joel 2:32).

graciously give us all things? . . . For I am convinced that neither death nor life, neither angels nor demons, neither the present nor the future, nor any powers, neither height nor depth, nor anything else in all creation, will be able to separate us from the love of God that is in Christ Jesus our Lord (Rom 8:31-32, 38-39).

Conclusion

Aren't you glad? I certainly am!

אֲדֹנָי

Adonai: Gracious Lord and Master

Reading: Judges 6:11-24

If you are attending for the first time, a brief orientation will help familiarise you with the key terms we are using in this series. For those who have been present for the first two sermons in the series, please pardon the repetition. The recap may just help to crystallise some of the concepts that are foundational to the series.

The Names of God

- In the Bible, names are extremely important
- They convey character
- In revealing himself to us, God has given us a number of names
- A knowledge of these names helps us to read the Bible in "high definition"
- More importantly, this will assist us to grow spiritually
- Every single one of us can easily discover what these names are

The Three Foundational Names

- "In the beginning, God (*Elohim*) created. . . ." (Gen 1:1)

- "Say to the Israelites, "The LORD (*Yahweh*) . . . has sent me to you. . . . This is my name forever" (Exod 3:15)

- "In the year that King Uzziah died, I saw the Lord (*Adonai*) seated on a throne. . . . (Isa 6:1)

Name	'Translation'	Main Emphasis
Elohim	God	Might
Yahweh	LORD	Faithful Presence
Adonai	Lord	Lordship
Yahweh Elohim	LORD God	Loving Power
Adonai Yahweh	Sovereign LORD	Gracious Lordship

This morning, as I read the passage (Judg. 6:11-24), I will use the Hebrew names for God, the LORD, and Lord (*Elohim, Yahweh*, and *Adonai*).

As some of us have discovered, debt can be a crippling. And not everybody who falls into debt has been downright irresponsible. In extreme circumstances, one may have to declare bankruptcy. And that, I am told, simplifies your life in one way and complicates it in several other ways. But it is a course of action open to one who is adjudged incapable of paying their debts.

In ancient Israel, bankruptcy, as we know it, was not an option. When a person fell into debt and could not possibly repay their creditors, they had to resort to an even less attractive course of action. They had to sell themselves into slavery. They became the property of their main creditor. They were at the disposal of their owner and he could do with them as he pleased. How terrible!

Actually, it was not quite as bad as it sounds. There were laws that forbade the inhumane treatment of slaves. I am not suggesting that slavery was ever a good system, but it does help us to realise that slavery in biblical days was not nearly as bad as slavery in more recent history. In fact, often slaves were very much better off than hired servants.

Where, Ellis, are you going with this? Well, I want you to envisage a young man who had fallen on hard times and had to sell himself into slavery. As a slave, he had to do exactly as he was told. He could be abused, terribly abused. There was no trade union for slaves to negotiate reasonable hours and favourable working conditions. At least a Hebrew slave knew that the Law of God decreed that after six years of service, his master had to release him. Not only that, he would not have to go away empty-handed; his master was instructed to supply him liberally from the flock, the threshing floor and the winepress. So, there was light at the end of the tunnel. After six years, he would regain his independence and he could make a fresh start as a free man.

Now imagine a really moving scene. The time has come for the slave to gain his emancipation. But he publicly renounces his right to freedom. During his enslavement, his master has been exceptionally kind and really good relationship has developed between the two of them. So he declares, "I love my master . . . and I do not want to go free" (Ex 21:5). Then, in a moving little ceremony, his master takes him to the door or the doorpost and pierces his ear with an awl. The man has chosen to be his servant for life.

Adoni
When the slave declared, "I love my master . . . and I do not want to go free," he used the Hebrew word *adoni*. It is a word that is used in the Bible to refer to an owner or a master. It is a term of respect. The word *adon* can be used as a general designation for a superior. It Modern Hebrew it means "Sir." When it refers, in the Bible, to a man it is always in the singular. It denotes lordship or ownership.

Adonai
It is highly significant that God is often referred to as *Adonai*. And almost always, when the term is used as a title for God, it is in the plural.[4]

---

[4] The Hebrew word *adon* means "lord" or "master." It is used to refer to a human master or owner, and only occasionally to refer to God (e.g. Ex. 23:17). The plural of this word is *adonim*—"lords" (e.g. Psa 136:3 Isa 26:13; Amos 4:1). *Adoni* is the singular form of the word with a 1st person possessive suffix (e.g. Judg. 6:13), hence "my lord." *Adonai* is the plural 1st person possessive and is invariably used to refer to God, even when the possessive "my" is not present.

This is really pertinent for us this morning. If fact, I believe we are touching on a matter that is crucial to our sense of well-being as Christians and to our effectiveness as a church. If we know God but fail to understand the implications contained in the name *Adonai*, we are missing the whole point. We may sense the disconnect between our profession and the quality of our lives. And we will certainly not be living the Christian life as it is meant to be lived. But it is a joy to live under the authority of *Adonai*. He is an infinitely wise and gracious Master.

AS *ADONAI*, GOD HAS A DOUBLE RIGHT TO OUR UNRESERVED ALLEGIANCE.

He is, after all, God, infinite in wisdom and perfect in holiness. Some people find it difficult to render such unconditional obedience to God because their picture of him is a caricature. They have transformed God into a cruel and capricious ogre. We do not bow before raw power. Just because he is mighty is not sufficient reason for us to defer to him. But God has revealed himself to us as a God of infinite goodness. He is worthy of our allegiance.

We have to think back of that slave who willingly and happily renounced his right to manumission. He believed he would know greater freedom living under the gracious and considerate care and oversight of his *adon* than he would living independently of him. He realised how much better off he would be in the service of his master than he would be attempting to paddle his own canoe.

But the primary reason we submit to God is loving gratitude. Peter reminds us that "it was not with perishable things such as silver and gold that (we) were redeemed . . . but with the precious blood of Christ, a lamb without blemish or defect" (1 Pet 1:18). He *set us free from the tyranny of sin and self-rule and invited us into the liberty of* *his service*. Paul loved to call himself a slave (*doulos*) of Christ Jesus. He states categorically, "Do you not know that your body is a temple of the Holy Spirit, who is in you, whom you have received from God? You are not your own; you were bought at a price" (1 Cor 6:19-20).

AS *ADONAI*, GOD MAY WELL CALL US TO AREAS OF SERVICE THAT ARE WAY BEYOND OUR SPHERE OF COMPETENCE.

Take the account of Gideon, about which we read a little earlier. These were dark days in Israel. Because of the waywardness of the Israelites, God allowed the Midianites to oppress them. The Midianites and their allies would wait until the Israelites had planted their crops and descend upon the region like a swarm of locusts and ravage the land. The situation was so bad that the Israelites crept into mountain clefts and caves to hide from their oppressors.

Then one day, **God appeared to a young man** who was threshing wheat in a winepress to keep it from the Midianites.

We may balk at Gideon's hesitation and his desire for signs of confirmation. But **when Gideon addressed his mysterious Visitor as *Adonai*, he meant it**. He risked his life by destroying his own father's altar to Baal and cutting down the Asherah pole beside it. In so doing he aroused the wrath of the entire community. They wanted to kill him.

He has asked, "How can I save Israel? My clan is the weakest in Manasseh and I am the least in my family." But the LORD answered, "I will be with you" (Judg. 6:15-16).

Yes, he politely asked for confirmation, but when God gave a clear instruction, even though it must have sounded ridiculous to him, he obeyed. At God's instruction he whittled down the army he had assembled from 32 000 to 10 000. Not very clever when you are up against a massive invading army. But at God's further instruction he reduced the army to 300 men. Gideon called God *Adonai—my Lord* and he meant it!

Several times we hear God call and commission his servants to undertake missions that are far above their natural capacity. Take Isaiah. When he has a vision of *Adonai*, seated on a throne, he exclaims, "Woe to me! I am ruined! For I am a man of unclean lips and I live among a people of unclean lips and my eyes have seen the King, *Yahweh Tsava'ōth* . . ." Then he heard the voice of *Adonai* saying, "Whom shall I send, and who will go for us?" He was being summoned to a task that was way above his competence, but it was *Adonai* who was speaking. So he said, "Here am I. Send me!"

When God calls young Jeremiah, he responds, "Ah *Adonai Yahweh*, I do not know how to speak; I am only a child." But God promises to be with him, touches his mouth and commissions him. When *Adonai* calls, he equips.

When God calls Ezekiel, he instructs him to announce to the obstinate nation, "This is what the Sovereign LORD (*Adonai Yahweh*) says . . ." (Ezek 2:4). From then on, Ezekiel repeatedly opens his prophetic messages with these words: "This is what *Adonai Yahweh* says (Ezek 3:11, 27 etc.).

So, it follows that . . .

WHEN *ADONAI* SPEAKS, THERE IS ONLY ONE APPROPRIATE RESPONSE.

We may not always understand. Like Peter we may have to say, "Master, we have worked hard all night and haven't caught anything. But because *you* say so, I will let down the nets" (Lk. 5:5).

What we have to do is to **make sure it is he who is speaking**. Once we have done that, it is not for us to second-guess the word of *Adonai*, the Lord.

And, of course, "Yes, Lord, I will do **anything** you say **except** . . ." is not an appropriate response! I cannot, at one and the same time say, "Yes Lord," and "except. . . ."

Kenneth Hemphill sums things up rather well when he says,

Throughout the Scriptures, those who know God as ***Adonai*** will always exhibit three characteristics:
1. They acknowledge themselves as servants [and] they count it a privilege to serve the living God.
2. They understand that their Master can supply all their needs.
3. [And] they realise that they can do whatever God calls them to do.[5]

WHEN WE CALL JESUS "LORD," WE ARE, IN FACT, RECOGNISING HIM AS *ADONAI*.

As we know, **the characteristic confession of the early church was "Jesus is Lord."** Although they honoured the emperor as king, they

---

[5] Kenneth Hemphill, The Names of God (Nashville, TN: Broadman and Holman Publishers, 2001), 32-33.

would rather die than say "Caesar is Lord (*Kurios; Adonai*)."[6] Paul could go as far as to say, "If you confess with your mouth, "Jesus is Lord," and believe in your heart that God raised him from the dead, you will be saved" (Rom 10:9).

We could even say that **Christians are those who acknowledge, in word and deed, that Jesus is Lord**.

Some make a sharp distinction between Jesus' role as Saviour and his role as Lord. Although it is less prevalent now, at one time there were many who proposed a two-phase Christian experience. They said something like this: when you first trusted Jesus, you accepted him as your Saviour, but that was not enough; you must now surrender to him and accept him as your Lord. They would point to numbers of great Christian men and women who had experienced a crisis moment in which they had surrendered to the Lordship of Christ. From then on, they had experienced a new dynamism.

Now, let me be crystal clear here. We cannot do that! Not for one moment would I question that these men and women, people like John Wesley, George Whitefield, and Charles Finney, had such an experience. My problem is with the interpretation that is foisted on these experiences and the tendency to place all the emphasis on a single experience and give it a particular name.

When you accepted Jesus into your life, you accepted him as *Saviour and Lord*! You cannot have him as your Saviour if you will not have him as your Lord. But here's what sometimes happens. We don't understand the full implications of our salvation at the time, nor do we appreciate all the implications of his Lordship. Then, one day,

---

[6] The confession, "Jesus is Lord," recognises his absolute authority. Christians are those for whom Jesus has the first word and the last word. The Greek word Kurios (Lord) is equivalent in this usage to the Hebrew word Adonai (Lord).

through the quiet prompting of the Holy Spirit, through a sermon or a study, through the help of a friend, or through a crisis in your life, you are challenged to make a deep-seated commitment, a surrender to his will. You realise that you have no business on the throne of your own life. In fact, there may be several such moments.

There is no need for us to adopt a cookie-cutter approach to this. God is much more imaginative than the paradigms we tend to create for him. But if, in all honesty, you find yourself in a position where your life in not submitted to the Lord, then your life is seriously out of kilter. You may be totally miserable or you may be relatively happy, but you will have lost the joy of your salvation, the inner joy that comes from living in submission to the will of Adonai.

Wherever we find ourselves, this morning, **the challenge of the Lordship of Christ comes to us afresh.** This is what was on Paul's mind when he addressed the Roman Christians. After describing the wonderful salvation provided for us through Christ, he appeals to us to live under his Lordship.

> I urge you brothers and sisters, in view of God's mercy, to offer your bodies as living sacrifices, holy and pleasing to God (Rom 12:1).

The mental picture of an altar of sacrifice was more familiar to Paul's original readers than it is to us. When a Hebrew worshipper brought his offering, say a lamb, to the Lord, he would come to the entrance of the tabernacle. As he made his way to the sanctuary, the animal was his. But then he would lay his hand on its head, so identifying himself with it. When he removed his hand, it was no longer his. He had willingly relinquished all rights to it. The dead (sacrificed) animal would be placed on the altar. When we present our bodies (ourselves) to God as living sacrifices, we relinquish all rights to self-governance.

Conclusion

It may be that he is calling you, for the very first time, to embrace him as your Lord and Saviour. Or, perhaps, you did present your body as a living sacrifice to him. You laid yourself on the altar, as it were, but *you have withdrawn your life from the altar.* You may need to present yourself to him afresh, this morning.

Once again, I need to emphasise that this is *all* good news. It's not as though the truth that Jesus is your Saviour is the good news and the requirement that he be your Lord is bad news. When a slave declared, "I love my *adoni*; I do not want to go free," it was a joyous occasion. Oh the joy of a life completely surrendered to the Lordship of Jesus! He **is** *Adonai* and we are always better off when we acknowledge him as such.

אֵל עֶלְיוֹן

El Elyon: God Most High

Readings: Genesis 14:17-24; Daniel 4:34-37; Isaiah 57:15

For the benefit of any who are walking in on this series on the names of God, and by way of reminder for those who have been in the other services, I need to make three comments: (1) God has revealed himself to us in a number of ways and his revelation is preserved for us in Scripture; (2) one of the ways in which he reveals himself is by giving us a number of names and compound names, and (3) if we remember that in Hebrew culture and in the Bible names convey meaning, then the names of God have to be highly significant.

We come to the first of the compound names of God: **El Elyon—God Most High**. As it is used in Scripture, it most certainly does not imply that there is a pantheon of gods and one of these outranks the others, so he is described as God *Most High*. There is only one God, and this is one of the ways in which he is described.[7]

We may understandably be tempted to imagine that the name is self-explanatory. It obviously refers to God's greatness and his majesty, to what theologians call his transcendence. So, for example, we could think of biblical phrases that affirm his exalted position like the one in

---

[7] It is true that *El* is the title of one of the Canaanite deities and that the name can be used generically to refer to deity. We are, however, looking at the biblical revelation. The clear equation of *El* (and *Elohim*) with *Yahweh* and the whole tenor of Scripture (especially in regard to foreign deities) precludes the notion that the patriarchs adopted a Canaanite deity. When the Israelites did serve the gods of the land they were roundly condemned for it.

Isaiah 55: "As the heavens are higher than the earth, so are my ways higher than your ways, and my thoughts than your thoughts" (Isa 55:9). At the dedication of his magnificent temple, Solomon stood in awe before God and prayed, "But will God really dwell on earth with human beings? The heavens, even the highest heavens, cannot contain you. How much less this temple I have built?" (2 Chron 6:18).

There is more to this name of God than the affirmation that he is great or that he is exalted above his creation. But we must, of course, start by affirming his greatness.

EL ELYON TOWERS HIGH ABOVE HIS CREATION. HE, AND HE ONLY, IS GOD.

He is inconceivably great.
We may look at the sheer magnificence of his creation and imagine how great and how 'imaginative' God must be.

This is confirmed when we see, in Scripture, how awe-inspiring his manifestations are.

The difference is not just one of degree; it is one of essential nature. The Danish philosopher, Søren Kierkegaard, spoke of the 'infinite qualitative distinction' between eternity and time, and between God and mankind.

Even the godliest of people, people like Moses, Isaiah, and Ezekiel, had to be shielded from the full manifestation of his glory, lest they die (Ex 33:20; Isa 6:5; Ezek 1:26-28).

No wonder the Teacher, in Ecclesiastes 5, cautions us: "Guard your steps when you go to the house of God. . . Do not be quick with your mouth; do not be hasty in your heart to utter anything before God.

God is in heaven and you are on earth, so let your words be few. . . . Therefore stand in awe of God" (Eccl 5:1, 2, 7).

This has to be our starting point when we talk about God. I become disturbed at the glibness with which some Christians speak of the Lord. It does not worry me so much when non-believers speak disrespectfully about "the man upstairs." They do not know him so an irreverent reference such as this is understandable. But one expects more reverence from God's people. There is a world of difference between intimacy and familiarity. I can never be genuinely intimate with God unless that intimacy is marked by a deep reverence. God is not my "buddy." In fact, we cannot appreciate grace unless we are convinced of God's greatness and his holiness. It is downgraded to a nondescript niceness. But when we start with God's majesty and greatness, then his grace is indeed "amazing grace."

But, as I hinted, the name *El Elyon* conveys more to us than the fact that God is inconceivably great. We are going to see this as we focus on two important Old Testament passages.

EL ELYON IS EXALTED ABOVE THE HEAVENS, BUT HE IS VERY MUCH INVOLVED IN EVENTS HERE ON EARTH.

The first mention of the name *El Elyon* is way back in the days of Abram.

Five city-states had been paying tribute to a powerful king by the name of Kedorlaomer. They had done so for twelve years but in the thirteenth year they rebelled. In the fourteenth year Kedorlaomer and the kings allied with him attacked the five rebellious city-states, among which were Sodom and Gomorrah. They utterly defeated the kings in the Dead Sea cities. They took prisoners and seized the goods of Sodom and Gomorrah.

One of the people taken captive was Abram's nephew Lot, who was living in Sodom.

When Abram heard the news, he rounded up 318 trained men and pursued the invading army as far as Dan, way up in the north. There he defeated the invading forces and retrieved the captives and the booty. That was quite an expedition since he was living in Hebron, south of Jerusalem.

No doubt this would have enhanced his status in the region.
As Abram returns with the people and the booty, he is met first by the king of Salem, which would later become Jerusalem, a man called Melchizedek, and then by the king of Sodom (Bera).

Melchizedek is described as priest of *El Elyon*--God Most High.
He is clearly an exceptional and a godly man. In Psalm 110, it is predicted that the priesthood of the Messiah will be patterned on the priesthood of Melchizedek. And the writer to the Hebrews explains how perfectly the priesthood of Melchizedek foreshadows that of Jesus (Heb 5: 5-10; 7:1-28).

He brought out bread and wine, blessed Abram in the name of God Most High and worshipped God Most High, Creator of heaven and earth, who had granted Abram victory. Abram recognised Melchizedek as a priest and gave him a tenth of everything.

The king of Sodom was a surly and presumptuous so-and-so. He said to Abram abruptly, "Give me the people and keep the goods for yourself." By the conventions of the day, he had no right to insist on anything. But Abram replied, significantly: "I have raised my hand to

Yahweh, El Elyon, Creator of heaven and earth, that I will accept nothing belonging to you, not even a thread nor the thong of a sandal, so that you will never be able to say, 'I made Abram rich'" (Gen. 14:22-24).

So, before we go any further, we can make three important observations:

El Elyon is declared to be the "Creator of heaven and earth." Since we know who created heaven and earth, we are in no doubt who is being referred to.

El Elyon and *Yahweh* are *declared* to be one and the same God by Abram, who raised his hand to *Yahweh, El Elyon*.

El Elyon is exalted as God Most High, but he is not reluctant to become directly involved in the affairs of his creatures. Clearly neither Melchizedek nor Abram was thinking of a distant, uninvolved God. For them "great" and "majestic" does not mean "distant." It was El Elyon who had given Abram success.

IN FACT, THERE IS NO AREA OF HUMAN EXISTENCE IN WHICH *EL ELYON* IS NOT INVOLVED.

The Babylonian Empire was one of the great empires of antiquity and its greatest king by far was Nebuchadnezzar. We read a fair amount about him in Scripture. None of what we read is more revealing than the account in Daniel 4.

The king was at home in his magnificent palace, contented and prosperous. Then he had a dream that shattered his serenity and disturbed him deeply. He saw an enormous tree standing in the middle of the land. It grew so large and strong that its top touched the sky and it became visible to the ends of the earth. Its leaves were beautiful, its fruit was abundant, and on it was food for all. Under it the animals found shelter and the birds lived in its branches.

Then a messenger from heaven descended and called out in a loud voice, "Cut down the tree and trim its branches; strip off its leaves and scatter its fruit. Let the animals flee from under it and the birds from its branches. But let the stump and its roots, bound with iron and bronze, remain in the ground. Let him be drenched with the dew of heaven, and let him live with the animals, among the plants of the earth. Let his mind be changed from that of a man and let him be given the mind of an animal till seven times pass by him."

None of his astrologers and enchanters could interpret it, so Nebuchadnezzar summoned Daniel, his trusted Hebrew official, and asked him to interpret the dream. Daniel was deeply troubled and said, "My lord, if only the dream applied to your enemies and its meaning to your adversaries. The tree you saw . . . was you, O king."

"This is the interpretation, O king, and this is the decree the Most High has issued against my lord, the king. You will be driven away from people and you will live with the wild animals; you will eat grass like cattle and be drenched with the dew of heaven. Seven times will pass by for you until you acknowledge that the Most High is sovereign over kingdoms on earth, and gives them to anyone he wishes."[8]

---

[8] Daniel 1:1 – 2:4a and 8:1 – 12:13 were written in Hebrew, and Daniel 2:4b – 7:28 was written in Aramaic, which was the common international language of the hear East at the time. It uses the same alphabet as Hebrew, is similar to but also different from it. The Aramaic word for Most High in Daniel 4:34-37 is *illaaya*, which is derived from the same root as the Hebrew *Elyon* and is identical in meaning.

Then Daniel appealed to Nebuchadnezzar: "Therefore, O king, be pleased to accept my advice: Renounce your sins by doing what is right, and your wickedness by being kind to the oppressed. It may be that your prosperity will continue."

A whole year went by and none of this happened. Then one day, as the king was walking on the roof of his royal palace, he said, "Is this not the great Babylon I have built as a royal residence, by my mighty power and for the glory of my majesty." And immediately the predictions of the dream were fulfilled. He lost his mind and was driven out. He ate grass like cattle. His hair became matted and resembled the feathers of an eagle and his nails looked like the claws of a bird.

At the end of that period he was restored. And here is what he declares:
> "I praised *the Most High*; I honoured and glorified him who lives forever.
> His dominion is an eternal dominion;
> His kingdom endures from generation to generation.
> All the peoples of the earth are regarded as nothing
> He does as he pleases with the powers of heaven
> And the peoples of the earth
> No one can hold back his hand
> Or say to him, 'What have you done?'
>
> Now I, Nebuchadnezzar, praise and exalt and glorify the King of heaven, because everything he does is right and all his ways are just. And those who walk in pride he is able to humble"
> (Dan 4:34,35).

Nebuchadnezzar, a Gentile king, discovered that "the Most High is sovereign over kingdoms on earth and gives them to anyone he wishes and sets over them the lowliest of people" (Dan 4:17). And it's not as though *El Elyon* concerns himself with certain matters and ignores others. He superintends *all* events.

This means that he has a plan for your life as well. Many of us almost think it's presumptuous to imagine that the Most High is concerned with 'little me', but it's not. *It's not about how important I think I am, but about who God has revealed himself to be.*

But life is such a mixture of good and evil, and it sometimes we cannot make head or tail of what is happening to us and to others. Bad things happen to good people. There is injustice which often seems to prevail. Can I really believe that God is in charge of everything? That's a legitimate question!

Now is not the time to launch into a discussion on what C. S. Lewis calls *The Problem of Pain* and John Wenham describes as *The Enigma of Evil*. Both of these authors give us some perspective on the problem and some clues to its resolution.

I remember reading of a letter to the editor of a local rag. A severe drought hit the land and the farmers were desperate. Many in the region were dedicated Christians so they called a day of prayer. They desperately needed the October rains, failing which their young plants would wither and die (in the southern hemisphere). One of the farmers in the neighbourhood refused to participate. That was his prerogative but he ridiculed his neighbours for their gullibility and insisted that God (if there was one) had absolutely nothing to do with agriculture.

Shortly after the prayer meeting the sky grew dark and it looked as though the rain was about to arrive. Instead, there was a devastating hail storm that destroyed the crops of the farmers. Strangely, the hail storm missed only one farm, almost as though it had been demarcated for protection. The farm belonged to the farmer who had refused to pray.

Not content to leaved it at that and thank his lucky stars for his good fortune, he wrote to the editor of the local newspaper, describing what had happened and citing the entire episode as proof of his thesis that either God did not exist at all or, if he did, he was not particularly interested in the fortunes or the prayers of his creatures. His tone was derisive and his attitude arrogant as he gloated over the refutation of the faith of his believing neighbours. For him this incident was decisive proof that religion was a waste of time. The editor published the letter in full, without amendment. At the end he added his editorial comment consisting of just fourteen words: "The Most High is under no obligation whatsoever to settle his accounts in October."

Once the great British preacher, W. E. Sangster, was approached by a distraught man who posed the agonised question, "Where was your God last night when they killed my son?" Sangster paused for a moment and then replied compassionately, "He was in exactly the same place last night as he was 2000 years ago when they killed his Son!"

As I said, it's a huge subject. All I will say here is that in this "as-yet-unredeemed-world" the Most High can allow the temporary continuance of evil without, in the least, forfeiting his sovereignty.

THE MOST WONDERFUL THING ABOUT *EL ELYON* IS "HIS CAPACITY TO BEND DOWNWARDS".[9]

It was *El Elyon* who created the heavens and the earth. It was *El Elyon* who enabled Abram to rescue his nephew Lot. It was *El Elyon* who gave the nations their inheritance when he divided all mankind (Deut 32:8). It is *Elyon* who invites us to call upon him in the day of trouble (Psa 50:14). No wonder the psalmist declares, "Whoever dwells in the shelter of *Elyon* will rest in the shadow of *Shaddai*. I will say of *Yahweh*, "He is my refuge and my fortress, *Elohay* (my God) in whom I trust (Psa 91:1-2). No wonder David could say, "I cry out to *El Elyon* who fulfils his purpose for me" (Psa 57:2).

When we say *"El Elyon"*, we are saying more than that God is highly exalted. He speaks through Isaiah: "For this is what the high and lofty One says—he who lives forever, whose name is holy: I live in a high and holy place, but also with him who is contrite and lowly in spirit" (Isa 57:15).

The involvement of *El Elyon* is seen most clearly in the person of Emmanuel (God with us), the One who took up residence among us as one of us. "In the beginning was the Word and the Word was with God, and the word was God. . . . And the Word became flesh and

---

[9] In his early years, Karl Barth, perhaps more than any other theologian, emphasised the transcendence and "otherness" of God. Later, he eloquently presented what he called "God's capacity to bend downwards." "God's deity is thus no prison in which He can exist only in and for Himself. It is rather His freedom to be in and for Himself but also with and for us, to assert but also to sacrifice Himself, to be wholly exalted but also completely humble, not only almighty but also almighty mercy, not only Lord but also servant, not only judge but also Himself the judged, not only man's eternal king but also his brother in time. And all that without in the slightest forfeiting His deity! He who does and manifestly can do all that, He and no other is the living God. Karl Barth, *The Humanity of God* (London: Collins, k1967), 46.

made his dwelling among us. We have seen his glory, the glory of the One and only who came from the Father full of grace and truth" (John 1:1, 14).

Conclusion
"Greatness" does not begin to describe what we mean when we call God *El Elyon*. We are speaking of more than power and more than moral perfection. We are referring to more than God's magnificence and his glory. We are certainly asserting that God is holy and loving. We start with the declaration that God is infinitely great, but we do not stop there. We celebrate the fact that he is involved with his world. As Nebuchadnezzar discovered, "the Most High is sovereign over earthly kingdoms." He is involved in your life and mine. *El Elyon* is the God who has gone to incredible lengths to be our Saviour. It is appropriate that we should bow before him with deep reverence. But there is more. He knows your name and sees your needs. He understands the deepest desires of your heart. Yes he is the Most High. He is above us, but "above" does not mean "distant." And it certainly does not mean "unconcerned." Let's renew our trust in him, not only as the one who rules over earthly kingdoms but as the one who really cares and is involved directly in our lives.

אֵל רֳאִי

El Ro'i: The God Who Sees Me

Readings: Genesis 16:1-16; 21:14-21

You may have heard about English teacher David McCullough's speech to the graduating class at Wellesley High School, in one of Boston's elite suburbs. It was delivered a few weeks ago and has subsequently gone viral on You-Tube. McCullough punctuated his speech with the statement, "Do not get the idea you are anything special, because you're not!" Lest they were in any doubt about his meaning he said, "Yes, you've been pampered, cosseted, doted upon, helmeted, bubble-wrapped. . . . But do not get the idea you're anything special, because you're not!"

It was a clever speech, full of subtle and sometimes not-so-subtle humour. McCullough urged the graduating seniors not to labour under the egotistical misapprehension that they are more important than they actually are. He appealed to them to make the world a better place. He made a good point and if we took his speech in the way he intended it, we can hardly argue with his contention.

But this morning I want to address a difficulty at the opposite extreme. Contrary to some of McCullough's audience of seniors, many of us may actually feel a dull sense of *unimportance*. It may be that the circumstances of your life have left you feeling that, in the total scheme of things, you don't matter very much. Why should you? You are one of millions, actually billions, of people.

And, if you and I are relatively unimportant on the human stage, how can we imagine that we mean something to God? He has important things to concern himself with and he keeps a pretty full schedule. Surely it is highly presumptuous for us to assume that you or I warrant his special attention.

Or you may be experiencing an acute sense of pain. You may have been discarded or rejected and you are in a lonely place—unnoticed by others! So why should you have the grandiose idea that God notices you. O sure, he is omniscient. He may see you in the same sense that he sees Jupiter or an amoeba, but does he notice you?

I HAVE TO WONDER HOW UTTERLY UNIMPORTANT HAGAR, THE MOTHER OF ABRAM'S FIRST SON, MUST HAVE FELT.

On the surface of things, she was the victim of a cruel set of circumstances.

Besides our two readings, she is mentioned in a cursory way in Genesis 25 and briefly in Galatians 4. So, we don't know a whole lot about her. Apparently, she was nobody special.

We know she was an Egyptian by birth and that she was Sarai's maidservant.

That means that Sarai probably acquired her when she and Abram went to Egypt to avoid the famine that had hit Canaan.

It is reasonable to surmise that she was considerably younger than Sarai and that the two of them enjoyed a good relationship—at least in the early days.

I have sometimes wondered how she had become a believer in the God of Abram and Sarai. And just how deep was her faith? She could hardly have lived as close as she did to Sarai and Abram without coming under their spiritual influence.

She, herself, may well have placed her trust in God, but she would have come to know about him through Sarai and Abram. Presumably, this had been one of the great benefits that had come her way. However it happened, she could count herself fortunate to have become the Sarai's attendant and possibly her confidant.

BUT ALL THAT WAS ABOUT TO CHANGE.

An Indecent Proposal
Almost twenty years ago, there was a movie appropriately named, "Indecent Proposal." Not exactly wholesome viewing, but I came across it on TV and I suspected that there was an important moral to the far-fetched and not-very-edifying story. A young couple, played by Woody Harrelson and Demi Moore, was in financial difficulty. Then a billionaire, played by Robert Redford, offered them $1 million if he could spend one night with the beautiful young wife. All I can recall is that succumbing to the indecent proposal caused major trauma and heartache. It really wasn't worth the million dollars.

The Souring of the Relationship
God had promised Abram a son and heir, but he'd been in Canaan ten long years and it seemed perfectly clear that Sarai was not able to bear children.

Ah, but there was a way to bring God's promise within the bounds of possibility. The customary law of the period provided them with an expedient. And when we want to give God a helping hand, we can usually find a convenient way to do so. Up to that point, there was nothing in God's promise that explicitly stated that *Sarai* had to be the biological mother. So why not opt for surrogate motherhood. If she gave Hagar to Abram, any child Hagar bore to Abram would legally be Sarai's child.

And so Hagar conceived. That's what Sarai wanted and that's what Sarai got. But the psychological and emotional consequences kicked in. Understandably Sarai felt nervous. The fact that Hagar had conceived so easily underlined the reproach of her own barrenness. And there was a new swagger about her maidservant's demeanour.

Oh my! Two's company but three's a crowd. The new edge to Hagar's behaviour was more than Sarai could take. No doubt Hagar was at least partly to blame. But sweet Sarai becomes angry and resentful and nasty. She turns on Abram. *"It's all your fault! I put my servant in your arms and now that she is pregnant, she despises me."*

Now you, like me, may be inclined to say, "Poor Abram. Caught in the middle!" But he should have known better. God may not have explicitly stated, at this stage, that Sarai would be the mother, but it was implicit and he must have known that. Even the great Abraham, friend of God and father of the faithful, can make a serious mistake. And did he pay for it?

Hagar's desperation
Abram knows the situation is serious, so he reminds Sarai that Hagar is *her* maid and appeals to her to do what is best. Sweet Sarai must have been absolutely awful. The word translated "mistreated" is the same word that is used to describe what the Egyptians later did to their Hebrew slaves. She made Hagar's life a total misery, so much so that the pregnant maid fled into the desert.

Just how she felt in that hot sun, pregnant, afraid, and heart sore, we can only imagine. She came to a spring where at least there was water. This may well have been the lowest point of her entire life.

The angel of Yahweh finds her.
Before we proceed, I need to point out that often when the Bible refers to the angel of the LORD, it is not referring to a regular angel. It rather refers to a special manifestation of God himself in angelic appearance. There is a note to this effect in the study guide together with some Bible references. Scholars refer to this as a theophany. You only have to read the references to verify that, on occasion, God did appear in this way.[10]

The Angel of *Yahweh* addressed her as "Hagar, servant of Sarai." He asked her, "Where have you come from and where are you going?"

"I am running away from my mistress Sarai," she answered.

---

[10] In this and some other passages where we read of the "Angel of Yahweh (the LORD)," reference is being made, not to an angel as such, but to an appearance of God in "angelic" form (Gen. 16:7, 13; 22:11-15; Ex. 3:2; Num 22:21-35; Judg. 2:1-5; 1 Kgs 19:3-9; 2 Kgs 1:3-4; Zech 3:1-9; 12:8). In other words, this is a theophany. Some commentators boldly describe such appearances as pre-incarnation appearances of the Son, the second Person of the Trinity. Passages such as this certainly incline us toward such a view.

This is the first reference in the Bible to the Angel of *Yahweh*. A few further comments may prove helpful. If we examine the references to him in the Old Testament, there is no doubt that he identifies himself with God. Those who met him believed that they had seen the LORD (e.g. Gen. 22:11 – 18; Ex. 3. 3:2-6; Judg. 6:11-22; Zech. 3:1-10). In addition there are instances where the *term* is not used but the person referred to carries the authority of God, (e.g. Gen. 32:22-32; Josh. 5:13-15). In fact, this is one of the great anticipations of the doctrine of the Trinity. Here is a divine person; he is identified with God and yet he seems to be distinct from God. It makes one think of John 1:1, "In the beginning was the Word and the Word was *with* God and the Word *was* God" (emphasis added). Significantly, we never read of *the* Angel of the Lord in the New Testament. The reason for this is simple: He is seated at the right hand of the Father as the ascended Lord Jesus Christ.

The angel of *Yahweh* told her, "Go back to your mistress Sarai and submit to her." He announced that he would increase her descendants so that they too would be too numerous to count.

Hagar's face
I wish I could have seen the look on Hagar's face: relief no doubt, but gratitude and awe as well. She has felt forsaken by those who have introduced her to God. Perhaps she had imagined that her good standing with God was dependent on her good standing with them. She was following *their* God and *they* have now rejected her. Where does that place her? But now, at her lowest point, God himself is speaking to her.

So she gave this name to *Yahweh* who spoke to her, "You are *El Ro'i* (the God who sees me)." She said, "I have now seen the One who sees me." For that reason she called the well "*Be'er Lahai Ro'i*--Well of the Living One who sees me."

Have you ever felt like that?
You have been let down by a Christian leader. Or just come to a low point and you wonder whether God sees or cares about you. You're "nobody special."

But when Hagar named *Yahweh*, *El Ro'i* she was not simply describing an incident in her life. She was saying something that is essential to the nature of God.

WE DO NOT SHOW UP SOMEWHERE IN GOD'S PERIPHERAL VISION; FOR GOD TO SEE IS TO CARE.

He does not take a quick, cursory glance at us. We are permanently in his field of vision. He does not see with the cold eye of an unconcerned omniscience. He sees with the caring eye of a Heavenly Father.

Think for a moment of some of the clear statements of Scripture.
> "I will instruct you and teach you in the way you should go; I will counsel you with my loving eye on you" (Psa 32:8).

> "But the eyes of the Lord are on those who fear him, on those whose hope is in his unfailing love. . . ." (Psa 33:18).

> Or, as Peter reminds us:
> "For the eyes of the Lord are on the righteous and his ears are attentive to their prayer" (1 Pet 3:12).

Let's continue the story

Hagar returns home. Ishmael is born. My guess is that there was considerable tension in the home but apparently there was truce of sorts. At last Abram had a son and a close relationship developed between him and his boy. And then, in one of history's amazing events, Isaac was born to ninety-year-old Sarah.

But things were about to turn sour again. At the feast held to celebrate Isaac's weaning, Sarah caught sight of Ishmael ridiculing her son Isaac. All the resentment of the past resurfaced. She insisted that Abraham get rid of Hagar and Ishmael. Abraham was devastated but God confirmed to him that the time had come for Hagar and Ishmael to leave. In what must have been a traumatic experience, Abraham provided Hagar with some provisions and sent her and Ishmael on their way.

God again sees and hears

Once again Hagar is in the desert around Beersheba, this time with the child she had been carrying when the Angel of *Yahweh* had appeared to her. Eventually they ran out of water. It is terribly hot in that area and it seemed certain that they could not survive. She could not bear to see her son die so she put him down under one of the bushes and sat down some distance away. Ishmael was afraid and, realising that this was probably the end, he began to sob.

Once again Hagar had reached the end of herself. My guess is that she was sobbing too. But just as God had seen and heard Hagar in her time of extremity a decade before, so he heard Ishmael's cry. He spoke once again: "What is the matter, Hagar? Do not be afraid; I have heard the boy crying as he lies there. Lift the boy up and take him by the hand, for I will make him into a great nation. God then opened her eyes and she saw a well of water and gave the boy something to drink. Once again God had proved that he both sees and hears in times of distress.

Does God see *you*?
You may be at a low point for some or other reason: rejection, illness, disobedience and the sense of guilt that you feel as a result of that disobedience. There could be a spiritual numbness; things are not as they once were.

Or you may just be one of many who believe that you don't warrant God's attention. Hagar could have felt like that. After all, though she was the mother of one of Abraham's children, she was only a maidservant. She may even have thought of herself as a second-class believer, an Egyptian who had somehow entered the kingdom via the back door. Now that she was away from the home of Abraham and Sarah, did *she* still matter to the God who had shown himself to be faithful to *them*? You may have thought that there are some special saints whose walk with the Lord is such that his eye is focused upon them. He hears their prayers and they seem to be on personal terms with him. But you are not sure he really *sees* you.

Conclusion

We tend to labour under a misapprehension: God has a very busy schedule and has more important things to attend to. We need to remember at all times, and especially at the low points in our lives, that we never pass from God's field of vision. Moreover, God does not see with the cold eye of an unconcerned omniscience. He sees with the watchful eye of a Heavenly Father. In comparison with the names of God we have considered so far, this name may seem quite ordinary: *El Ro'i*, the God who sees me. But it's far from ordinary when you are in the desert and at your wit's end. When you are at the point of extremity, there is one thing you need to know more than anything else in the world: *El Ro'i*—"You are the God who sees me."

And this does not apply only in times of extreme need. We may not always be aware of it, but God's gracious eye is always upon us. He did not suddenly turn his attention towards Hagar when she was languishing in the desert. It was then that *she became aware* of her need and it was at that point that she declared, perhaps to her surprise, but certainly to her joy: "*'Attāh El Ro'i*: You are the God who sees me."

אֵל שַׁדַּי

"*El Shaddai:* The All-Sufficient God"

Readings: Genesis 27:46-28:5; Ruth 1:1-5, 19-22

For those who are here for the first time today, and by way of reminder for those who have been attending over the last two months, let me make a few comments. In describing to us who he is, God has made him known by giving us a number of names and compound names. This is very important when we realise that in the cultural setting in which the Bible was written, names conveyed character; they were intended to reveal who a person was, what they were really like. With a little help all of us can identify the names of God in our English translations of the Bible.

Nine years ago I purchased a state of the art TV set. I still have it. But so much has happened in the world of TV technology. My TV is just fine, until I have had a spell watching a high-definition television. But once I have watched the BC Lions or the Canucks in HDTV, my old TV looks a bit dull and indistinct. In a sense, an awareness of the names by which God has revealed himself enables us to read the biblical accounts in high definition.

Today we are going to encounter a name of God that helps us to see several passages in high definition. We do need to identify it so that you can find it in our translation of the Bible.

As we read two well-known passages today, we will encounter the name El Shaddai.

***EL SHADDAI* IS THE BEST KNOWN AND PROBABLY THE MOST LOVED OF THE COMPOUND NAMES OF GOD.**

It occurs no fewer than forty-eight times in the Hebrew Bible; thirty-one of these occurrences are in the Book of Job alone.

I have to tell you that I agree with those scholars who are not entirely happy with the translation, "God Almighty." The name *El Shaddai* tells us more than that God is Almighty. But it is difficult to find a single word to substitute for the word Almighty.

There are two complementary ways in which we ascertain what a name like this means.

The first is etymology. In other words, we ask, "Is there anything in the word or words that give us a clue. So if the name is formed from a particular root or stem, this may well give us an indication regarding its meaning.

The other way is for us to examine its usage throughout Scripture. What is happening when that name is mentioned or invoked? What nuance is being highlighted?

Here's what we are going to do this morning. I am not going to tell you right now what I think the name means. Rather we will travel together and draw some conclusions as we go along. Let's build a step at a time.

A POIGNANT MOMENT.

The first time we read the name is in relation to the promise God had made to Abram. When he called Abram to leave his homeland, his people and his family, God promised that he would make of him a great nation (Gen. 12:1-3). For years Abram and Sarai had no child. God reaffirmed the promise in more specific terms when he later assured Abram that "a son coming from his own body would be (his) heir" (Gen. 15:4). The years dragged on and both Abram and Sarai gave up hope. Then, when Abram was 99 (and Sarai just 10 years younger), *Yahweh* appeared to him and said, "I am *El Shaddai*. . . . I will confirm my covenant between me and you and will greatly increase your numbers. . . ." (Gen. 17:1, 2). So, our first introduction to God as *El Shaddai* is in the context of his faithfulness. He stands by his word even when the fulfilment of the promise seems impossible.

But there's more. There was tension between Isaac's two sons, Esau and Jacob. No wonder! They were fraternal twins and there had been rivalry between them from the womb. Jacob had deceived his father, who was virtually blind, into giving him Esau's blessing. This wasn't the first time there had been a run-in between the boys. Esau, the more rugged of the two, bore a grudge and was waiting for Isaac to die before he murdered Jacob. So Isaac's wife Rebekah knew she needed to place Jacob beyond Isaac's reach. Esau's wives had been a source of grief to Isaac and Rebekah. So she appealed to Isaac to send Jacob to the place of her birth, Harran, on the pretext of finding a suitable wife.

Isaac reluctantly agreed. He was convinced he did not have long to live. Rebekah's homeland was far away and he thought he would probably never see Jacob again. He knew that God's promise to Abraham and him were to be fulfilled through Jacob.

Partings can be hard at the best of times. This one was particularly difficult. No international airport in Beersheba, no email, no Skype. Will he ever see his son again? It must have been a profoundly moving experience as Isaac blessed Jacob and takes his leave of him. Listen to him as he commits his son to the LORD for protection and blessing:

> May *El Shaddai* bless you and make you fruitful and increase your numbers until you become a community of peoples. May he give you and your descendants the blessing given to Abraham, so that you may take possession of the land where you now live as an alien, the land God gave to Abraham (Gen. 28:3-4).

It seemed natural for Isaac to invoke the name of *El Shaddai* when he committed his son Jacob to God's care. He is the one who made the promises, who stands by his word, the one who provides and protects.

Years later, when Jacob eventually returned to Canaan, God met with him at Bethel and said, "I am *El Shaddai*; be fruitful and increase in number. . . ." (Gen. 35:11). God restated the promises he had made previously regarding his blessing and Jacob's descendants and the land.

We haven't examined all the references, but we can draw at least a provisional conclusion. It seems that *El Shaddai* is a God of infinite resourcefulness and tenderness, one who is faithful to his word, one who watches over his children and delights in imparting the best gifts to them. But that interim inference is about to be tested.

APPARENTLY *EL SHADDAI* DOESN'T ALWAYS PROTECT HIS CHILDREN AND PROVIDE FOR THEM.

Several hundred years pass. It seems that God has certainly kept his promises—*some* of them. Jacob's decedents have multiplied. God has brought them out of Egypt and given them the land he promised to them. But among other things, a severe famine breaks out in the land, so much so that people are starving. Our attention is focussed on one family in particular.

A man called Elimelech is living in a place called Bethlehem with his wife Naomi and their two sons, Mahlon and Kilion. But the famine is so severe that they have to leave Bethlehem and travel around the Dead Sea to the land of Moab.

While they are in Moab, the two sons marry Moabite women, but tragedy strikes. Elimelech dies, and so do Mahlon and Kilion. *Three widows!* And the plight of a widow in those days was grim to say the least.

By the way, you can see how names have significance. Bethlehem means "the House of Bread." There was famine in the house of bread. Elimelech means "My God is King." He dies, as do his two sons. Naomi means "Pleasantness."

Think of how Naomi felt as she dragged herself back to the Promised Land with a broken heart. Their arrival in Bethlehem was big news and the women of the town exclaimed, "Can this be Naomi?" Her response was highly significant.

> 'Don't call me Naomi ('Pleasant'),' she told them. Call me Mara ('Bitter'), because the Almighty (*Shaddai*) has made my life very bitter. I went away full but the LORD (*Yahweh*) has brought me back empty. Why call me Naomi? The LORD (*Yahweh*) has afflicted me; the Almighty (*Shaddai*) has brought affliction upon me" (Ruth 1:20-21).

Can you hear the pain in Naomi's voice? It's bad enough to lose your husband and your two sons. But if *Shaddai*, the One who protects and watches over us with tender love, afflicts us, we have to feel wretched indeed.

IN FACT, IT MAY SEEM AS THOUGH HE IS DOING THE EXACT OPPOSITE.

We encounter the same thought in Job. In fact, the name *El Shaddai* or *Shaddai* occurs 48 times in the entire Old Testament and 31 of these occurrences are in the Book of Job alone.

Here was a righteous man who served God with all his heart and enjoyed prosperity. He had good reason to trust in Yahweh and to celebrate the fact that he is *El Shaddai*. If *Shaddai* is the One who protects, Job and his family knew protection. If he is the One who provides, Job was exceptionally wealthy. And every morning as he prayed, he could give thanks to *El Shaddai*, the God of abundance and compassion. He could sing the little Gaither song, "God is good, all the time."

Then, suddenly and without warning, his entire world crashed around his ears. He lost not only his possessions but his children and his health. *We*, as the readers, are given an insight into what was going on behind the scenes. The first *he* knew about it was when his servants came running from every direction to deliver one element of bad news after another. We see him on the dunghill, full of festering sores, and yet clinging steadfastly to his faith.

Then three of his friends, the notorious Job's comforters, arrived. They appeared to be comforting him but added insult to his injury by insinuating that he must have been guilty of secret sin to have suffered so much. So Eliphaz, the oldest of the three, could trot out religious phrases in defence of God, or so he thought: *"Blessed is the man whom God corrects,"* he says, *"so do not despise the discipline of Shaddai"* (Job 5:17).

In answer to his insensitive friends Job poured out his complaint. At the heart of his anguish was the fact that he could no longer understand God. What he was experiencing was contradicting all he knew about God. He had known God as *El Shaddai*.

But Job was experiencing oppression that was almost unbearable. He explained why his pain was so intense:

> If only my anguish could be weighed
> And all my misery placed on the scales!
> It would surely outweigh the sand of the seas –
> No wonder my words have been impetuous.
> The arrows of *Shaddai* are in me,
> My spirit drinks in their poison;
> God's terrors are marshalled against me. (Job 6:1-4)

Like Naomi, Job could not understand how *Shaddai* could turn against him. It seemed totally out of character. That was Job's greatest problem. Imagine a child with an attentive and compassionate mother. Her words are always positive and encouraging. Her correction is firm but gentle and instils a sense of security. He looks to her for provision and finds that she never disappoints him. She is always present to protect him and the relationship is excellent. Then suddenly she undergoes an inexplicable change of personality. She brutalises her son, adding vicious physical beatings to psychological abuse. The child's world caves in. He cries himself to sleep at night. The welts on his body are ugly but that is not the major problem. He cannot understand the change of mood. The person who had been so dependable and to whom he looked for love has gone berserk. When a compassionate and dependable mother behaves like that, panic and confusion are understandable. And that is how Job felt. *Shaddai* seemed to have made him a target. Nothing could be more painful than that.

SO WHAT CAN WE SAY ABOUT SHADDAI? MORE PARTICULARLY, WHAT CAN YOU EXPECT FROM HIM? HOW DOES THIS IMPACT YOU?

We are given no guarantee that life will be trouble-free.

The lie of the so-called "faith (prosperity) movement." The "bible" they read is a reduced canon of selected verses yanked out of context. We need the perspective of the whole of Scripture. I have a pastoral concern. Sincere Christians can be seriously hurt. I've seen it happen!

We are given the assurance that no matter what happens to us, God is and remains *El Shaddai*. He does care. He will protect. His promises can be trusted. He provides. He is all-sufficient.

I earlier mentioned etymology. When we look at the composition of a compound term or the root of a Hebrew word, it gives us a clue? A few suggestions have been made relative to the word *El Shaddai*. A few commentators have suggested that the word Shaddai is derived from a word meaning "to devastate" or "to overpower." Hardly likely! Others have linked it with an Akkadian word meaning "mountain." That too seems a long shot.

One suggestion does merit closer attention. The Hebrew word for breast is *shad*. In fact the name *Shaddai* and the word for breasts occur in the same verse: We are told that Joseph will prosper because of *Shaddai* who blesses him with the blessings of heaven above, blessings of the deep that lies below, blessings of the breast (*shadayim*) and the womb" (Gen. 49:25). That does not settle the matter, but it is consistent with all that is said about *Shaddai*.

Breasts were a symbol of care, and comfort, and provision. This has emboldened some preachers to speak of the "mother love of God." We know that humankind was created in the image of God. And whatever aspects of the image of God remain in us are to be found in humankind, male and female.

Through the fall, the image of God was marred but not completely obliterated. Here and there we see glimpses of the divine image. If we see it anywhere at all we see it in the instinct of mother love, the instinct of a mother to love unconditionally, to protect at any cost, to sacrifice and to provide for the infant at her breast.

So, what if you are trusting El Shaddai, the One who provides and protects, the one who keeps his promises, the God of infinite resourcefulness, the all-sufficient God? And things are not going too well?

All I would suggest is this. You heard Naomi when she arrived back in Bethlehem, bereft of her husband and her two sons, a distraught widow without any means of financial support. But suppose you could have spoken to Naomi some time later. By this time she is living in the spacious home of her kinsman Boaz, who has married her faithful daughter-in-law, Ruth. Naomi is caring for Ruth's little son, Obed, as if he were her own child. Her life is filled with joy and meaning!

And suppose you could speak to her today. You could tell her that something has happened that is far greater than she could ever have imagined possible. Little Obed grew up and fathered a son. His name was Jesse. And Jesse grew up and fathered a son who was called David, King David! So, in a small but significant way, Naomi was instrumental in the coming of the One who was called "the Son of David."

You know what she would say? "Do not call me Mara ("Bitter"); *call me Naomi* ("Pleasant"), because *Shaddai* has made my life very rich. I came back empty, but Yahweh has given me abundance. Why call me Mara? *Yahweh* has watched over me; *Shaddai* has showered blessing upon me" (Inversion of Ruth 1:20-22).

So we would say *El Shaddai* is the *All-sufficient God*, the compassionate God, the God of all grace who provides and protects and blesses and keeps his promises. That's who he is. It may not have seemed like it to Abram or to Naomi or to Job, but that's who he is.

One more thing; one more important thing! The character of God as *El Shaddai* is seen most perfectly in Jesus. Look at his compassion! He is the One who invites those who are burdened and heavy-laden to come to him and find rest for their souls. God shall supply all our needs according to his glorious riches in Christ Jesus. I could go on. Nowhere is the character of *El Shaddai* seen more clearly than in the person of our Lord Jesus Christ.

Conclusion
Wherever you find yourself, riding the crest of a wave? God is *El Shaddai* and he blesses us. Or perhaps in a bad place and things are not good? God is still *El Shaddai,* he remains the same. In the long term we see his faithfulness. He is good all the time even when we don't experience it. So whatever your particular position the invitation to actively trust him wherever you are, the one who is *El Shaddai*.

אֵל עוֹלָם

El Olam: the Everlasting God.

Readings: Genesis 21:22-34; Isaiah 40:27-31

Have you ever wondered why it is that God always just existed? I have. And I suppose that most of us have gone down that road at some stage. And if you ponder it for any length of time, you run into a mental brick wall. It almost feels as if your brain 'hurts'.

We are not going to spend too much time pondering this question this morning. I once heard someone trying to explain the duration of eternity in a way the children could understand it. He asked the audience to think of a mountain like Mount Baker. Imagine that a sparrow comes to it, perches on the summit for a second or two and then flies off. A thousand years later a sparrow does the same (I think it's reasonable to assume that it is a different sparrow). This happens just once every thousand years. When Mount Baker has been completely worn away by the fleeting, millennial visits of the sparrows, the second of the first day of eternity will have just begun. Of course, the explanation is inadequate because it can only attempt to explain eternity in terms of time.

As I said, I am not going to spend this morning's sermon wrestling with this brainteaser, but allow me to make a suggestion that may be of help to some of us. We certainly can't explain why God should always have existed, but I think we can at least appreciate why we can't explain God's "origin". We can explain why we can't explain why God was always "there".

In this information age, our personal computers perform a whole host of complicated functions with ease, so much so that some almost attribute intelligence and personality to these machines. The key is in the programming. We may not like the comparison but, in a sense, we too have been "programmed," programmed to operate in the finite realm of time and space. We are certainly not just automatons but our minds are wired to live in a finite world. An important part of this wiring is the notion of cause and effect. We know, almost instinctively, that every effect has to have a cause (quantum mechanics notwithstanding). This law applies to everything we know--*in the finite world,* that is. And when we attempt to cross over into the infinite realm, our minds protest: God cannot just always have been there. He too must have been "caused." We cannot cope with the concept of an eternally existing person, not because the idea is inherently defective, but because our "programmed" minds tell us God must also have been caused. As Kenneth Hemphill states, "We have been taught that everything that exists has to have a prior cause. . . . God is the uncaused cause. He is the first cause and before him there was no other and after him there will be no other. Life is found in him."[11]

It may be difficult or impossible to get our minds around the idea of God's eternality, but the *alternative is even more problematic.* Given the fact of our own existence, it is particularly difficult to conceive of an "eternal nothingness," and to imagine that nothing gave rise to something.

But this is not where the emphasis of Scripture lies when it speaks of God as *El Olam.* It simply declares that God is eternal. He has always existed and he will always exist. It does not try to explain his eternality. God describes himself to Moses as "I AM" (Ex 3:14). The

---

[11] Kenneth Hemphill, The Names of God (Nashville, TN: Broadman and Holman Publishers, 2001), 66

prophet Isaiah asks: "Do you not know? Have you not heard? The LORD is the everlasting God, the creator of the ends of the earth" (Isa 40:28). In the Book of Revelation, God says, "I am the Alpha and the Omega, who is and who was and who is to come, the Almighty" (Rev 1:8). And, the writer to the Hebrews insists that "whoever comes to God must believe that he exists and that he rewards those who earnestly seek him" (Heb 11:6).

When the Bible speaks of God as *El Olam*, its focus is on far more than the fact that he is without beginning or end. It's not simply about the duration of existence. It deals with a concrete reality, not an abstract concept. And it relates God's eternity to our circumstances here and now. It is because he is eternal that God is dependable, he is consistent, and he is faithful.

FAITHFULNESS IN VIEW.

The Incident
The first reference to God as *El Olam* occurs in Genesis 21 and almost takes us by surprise. Abimelech, the Philistine king of Gerar, approaches Abraham. He sees the necessity, both for himself and his descendants, of establishing cordial relationships with this nomadic foreigner. If fact, he wants Abraham to swear to him that he will continue to deal kindly with him and his descendants. Abraham has no hesitation in agreeing, and placing himself under oath. He raises the matter of a well of water that had been seized by Abimelech's servants. That matter is resolved, Abraham gives sheep and cattle to Abimelech and the two men make a treaty. They call the place Beersheba (Well of the Oath) and Abimelech and his general return to the land of the Philistines.

Then, Abraham plants a tamarisk tree and calls upon the name of the LORD, the Eternal God: *Yahweh, El Olam*.

Tame?

On the surface of things, amidst the high drama that precedes and follows this event, it seems rather tame. But it is included for a reason. It obviously has spiritual significance, especially the fact that Abraham sees this as a moment to commemorate by planting a tamarisk tree and calling on the name of *Yahweh El Olam*. He seems to have seen this as an important milestone in his life.

If ever a man had reason to feel that he was transient, Abraham did. He was living in the land of promise but he was living in tents as an alien. God had promised him the whole land, but he did not even own a square foot of it (Acts 7:5). The writer to the Hebrews puts it so well: "[Abraham] made his home in the promised land, like a stranger in a foreign country; he lived in tents as did Isaac and Jacob, who were heirs with him of the same promise" (Heb 11:8-10). He has learned to trust in God alone, despite appearances to the contrary, for the fulfilment of the promises. Now one of the powerful local kings recognizes the permanence of the Abrahamic family in the land ("God is with you in everything you do" [Gen. 21:22]). Abimelech sees the importance of making a treaty with him. The thought of God's constancy, his faithfulness, must surely have been in Abraham's mind. So it was appropriate that he worship the Eternal God who had remained true to his promises. In other words, the fulfilment of God's promises in time is related to the fact that he is *El Olam*, the Eternal God. If there is one thing Abraham had learned about God it is that he can be trusted to keep his promises. He learned this the hard way. At times it didn't seem like it, but El Olam is faithful; he *always* keeps his promises.

CLEARLY THIS NAME IS GIVEN NOT SO MUCH TO ENGAGE OUR MINDS BUT TO ENCOURAGE OUR HEARTS.

Yes, our minds boggle as we contemplate God's eternity. In fact there is no such thing as eternity outside of God. If God, and only God, is eternal, there is no such thing as "eternity" as an abstract entity apart from God. This emboldened Karl Barth to say:

> It is the living God himself. It is not only a quality which he possesses. It is not only a space in which he dwells. . . . We cannot for one moment think of eternity without thinking of God, nor can we think of it otherwise than by thinking of God. . . . Eternity is the living God himself.[12]

This is closer to where the accent of Scripture lies. Its accent is on character, not duration. It celebrates the fact that God is completely consistent and completely faithful. He declares, through the prophet Malachi, "I, *Yahweh*, do not change" (Mal 3:6). James assures us that "Every good and perfect gift comes down from above, from the Father of heavenly lights who does not change like shifting shadows" (Jas 1:17).

This has some important implications for us in the good times and in the bad. When an unexpected crisis arises, when seeming tragedy strikes, when you cannot make head or tail of your circumstances, it is important to know that God is faithful. Even when life seems relatively uneventful, it is important to know God as *El Olam*.

---

[12] Karl Barth, *Church Dogmatics,* ed. G. W. Bromiley, and T. F. Torrance, vol. 2, *The Doctrine of God*, pt. 1, trans. T. H. L. Parker, W. B. Johnston, Harold Knight, and J. L. M. Haire (Edinburgh: T & T Clark, 1957), 638.

We can draw two important inferences from this truth:
You and I can have absolute certainty regarding the future.

Doubt
I still meet quite a few genuine Christians who have nagging doubts about the future. Perhaps something will go wrong. Maybe we will deviate from the path and lose our salvation. Can we really believe what God tells us about the future? What if he changes his mind or if things just do not turn out as they are depicted in Scripture? In the face of such doubts it is important to remember . . .

Your salvation did not take God by surprise.
It helps to know that your salvation is rooted in the faithfulness of *El Olam*. Let me put this crudely to make a point. God did not wake up one morning to discover, to his surprise, that you had committed your life to him. God, of course, always works on Greenwich Mean Time, as every good Brit knows, so your conversion took place during our daytime but it was his night time. You know that's not true, but neither is it true, in any sense, that your salvation took him by surprise.

Listen to Paul as he encourages Timothy. "[God saved us] and called us to a holy life, not because of anything we have done but because of his own purpose and grace. This grace was given us in Christ Jesus *before the beginning of time* but has now been revealed through the appearing of our Saviour, Christ Jesus" (2 Tim 1:9-10; emphasis added).

And he writes to Titus along the same lines. He speaks of our "faith and knowledge [that rest] on the hope of eternal life, which God, who does not lie, promised *before the beginning of time*" (Titus 1:2; emphasis added).

To the Ephesians he says, "[God] chose us in him (Christ) *before the creation of the world* to be holy and blameless in his sight" (Eph 1:4; emphasis added).

In that beautiful song in Romans 8, he says,
> "And we know that in all things God works for the good of those who love him, who have been called according to his purpose. ^{29} For those God foreknew he also predestined to be conformed to the image of his Son, that he might be the firstborn among many brothers and sisters. ^{30} And those he predestined, he also called; those he called, he also justified; those he justified, he also glorified" (Rom 8:28-30).

Part of an Eternal Plan
Again I bow before mystery. (We do not attempt to take our position in eternity behind God and look over his shoulder down through human history. Those who do so easily distort the biblical teaching on God's grace). We know that he has called us here and now to be his children. And then we discover that this did not just happen "out of the blue'. We have been on his mind for all eternity. Someone tried to explain how this works. He said: "It's as though, as a non-believer, I saw an archway and on it were written the words, 'Whosoever will-- to the Lord may come.' And I decided to follow Jesus. I entered through the archway and took my first baby steps as a Christian. When I looked back, I saw words written on the believers' side of the archway: 'Chosen before the foundation of the world.'"

Confidence does not Lead to Carelessness.
In 1937, when money was worth a whole lot more than it is today, San Francisco's famous Golden Gate Bridge was completed at a cost of $77 million. During the construction of the first part of the bridge no safety devices were used and 23 men fell to their death in the waters far below. In the construction of the second part, it was

decided to install the greatest safety net in the world even though the cost amounted to $100 000 (millions in today's currency). It saved the lives of nineteen men who fell into it without injury. Significantly they became known as the "Half-Way-to-Hell Club." In addition, the work went on from 15 to 25% faster with the men relieved from the fear of falling to their deaths. The knowledge that they were secure left the men free to devote their energies to the particular tasks at hand. For the true believer confidence does not lead to carelessness.

We not only find hope for the future; we derive strength in the present.

El Olam: The God who is with us in the Present
Again Karl Barth makes an insightful comment on the significance of God's eternity for us: "Rightly understood, the statement that God is eternal tells us what God is, not what He is not. . . . As the eternal One he is present personally at every point of our time. As the eternal One it is he who surrounds our time and rules it with all that it contains." (Psa 139)[13]

The passages that draw attention to the fact that God is *El Olam* do not encourage us to ignore the realities and challenges of the present and focus on the "sweet by and by when we shall meet on the beautiful shore." This is not escapism or some kind of compensatory belief: "it may be tough in time but there's always eternity". On the contrary, *El Olam* is the One who promises to be with us at every point of the present.

---

[13] Ibid., 613.

In the Difficult Moments

For one or other reason, we may find ourselves in distress. An unexpected development gives rise to concern and consternation. Our mortality looms large. That's how the author of Psalm 102 felt: "My days vanish like smoke; my bones burn like glowing embers . . . my days are like the evening shadow; I wither away like grass" (Psa 102:11). But he turned to *El Olam*, the Eternal God, in prayer: "But you, O LORD, sit enthroned forever (*l'olam*); your renown endures through all generations. You will arise and have compassion on Zion, for it is time to show favour to her; the appointed time has come" (Psa 102:12).

Or we become acutely conscious of our frailty. We may wonder whether God really cares. Isaiah challenges us.

> Why do you say . . . 'My way is hidden from the LORD;
> my cause is disregarded by my God'?
> Do you not know?
> Have you not heard?
> The LORD (*Yahweh*) is the Everlasting God (*Elohim Olam*)
> He will not grow tired or weary,
> And his understanding no one can fathom.
> He gives strength to the weary
> And increases the power of the weak.
> Even youths grow tired and weary,
> and young men stumble and fall;
> But those who hope in the LORD
> Will renew their strength.
> They will soar on wings like eagles;
> They will run and not grow weary,
> They will walk and not be faint (Isa 40:27-31).

Or you may simply be bewildered by the pace of change. In his best-selling book, *Future Shock*, written over 30 years ago, Alvin Toffler describes what he calls the "epidemic of change." "Change," he says, "is avalanching upon our heads and most people are grotesquely unprepared to cope with it. . . Future shock is the dizzying disorientation brought on by the premature arrival of the future."

The psalmist asks, "When the foundations are being shaken, what can the righteous do?" The response is the same in our day as it was in his: "The LORD is in his holy temple; the LORD is on his heavenly throne" (Psa 11:3-4).

So when we are struck by the fleeting nature of life; when we experience disappointment or disillusionment or fatigue; when we struggle through the night of time with its contradictions and its reversals; then we can thank God that, even in time, we know him as *El Olam*--the Eternal God. We rejoice that the One who was chosen before the foundation of the world, was revealed in these last days for our sakes (I Pet. 1:20). We remember that he said, "Before Abraham was, I AM" (John 8:58). We know that "he is the same yesterday, today and forever" (Heb. 13:8). He is "the Alpha and the Omega, the First and the Last, the Beginning and the End" (Rev. 22:13; cf. 1:8, 17). It certainly helps in time to know the One who is eternal.

יְהוָה יִרְאֶה

Yahweh Yireh: The LORD will Provide

Readings: Genesis 22:1-14; Romans 8:32

The first and best known of the compound names of *Yahweh*. It is celebrated in the song Jehovah Jireh. (Charles Price, Peoples' Church Channel 10)

> **JEHOVAH JIREH**
> My provider
> His grace is sufficient
> For me, for me, for me
> Jehovah Jireh
> My provider
> His grace is sufficient for me
>
> My God shall supply all my needs
> According to his riches in glory
> He will give His angels
> Charge over me
> Jehovah Jireh cares
> For me, for me, for me
> Jehovah Jireh cares for me

It has a folksy beat and it certainly contains important biblical truth. If the song has a weakness, it is that it can so easily be sung in self-centered way. It could lend itself to the idea that God is a cosmic Santa Claus. As the infinite benefactor he supplies our needs. He most certainly does, sometimes in the most remarkable ways. But, in the process of celebrating this reality we may trivialise the truth. But the reality conveyed by this name is much, much, much more wonderful than that.

SO LET'S SEE HOW MUCH MORE THE NAME CAN MEAN TO US.

The story is well known but often important details are missed, so let me briefly recount it. Interestingly Richard Dawkins and Christopher Hitchens, two of the most prominent atheists, find this particularly scandalous and offensive and pure fiction. They think that Isaac had a permanent psychological scar as a result of the event even though they don't believe it. If you don't understand the biblical spiritual sense of the passage, you might as well not read it. You realise that they actually miss the point of the passage entirely.

THE STORY

"Laughter" in the home
There was laughter in the home of Abraham and Sarah. For years God has promised that they would have a son and his promises were to be centred on this boy, but there was no son.

After going down a number of futile cul-de-sacs, God speaks to 100 year old Abraham and tells him that Sarah is going to bear him a son. Abraham's reaction is not irreverent but falls face down and bursts out laughing. Too improbable. When Sarah hears the news, she too laughs. It is interesting that Isaac's name means laughter.

The Enigmatic Command:
In an instant God wipes the smile off Abraham's face that contradicts all that he knows about God and his promise. God tells him:
> "Take your son, your only son, whom you love—Isaac—and go to the region of Moriah. Sacrifice him there as a burnt offering on a mountain I will show you."

It interesting that when God addresses Abraham, he responds with "Here am I". That is more than just a yes. English doesn't adequately translate the Hebrew word. Literally it means, "I'm here", but also attentive and receptive to the command. The amazing command is to sacrifice the son of promise.

Remarkable: No hint of hesitation
> *"Early the next morning Abraham got up and loaded his donkey. He took with him two of his servants and his son Isaac. When he had cut enough wood for the burnt offering, he set out for the place God had told him about."*

How do you think Abraham felt?

Mount Moriah
> *"On the third day Abraham looked up and saw the place in the distance.* [5] *He said to his servants, "Stay here with the donkey while I and the boy go over there.* **We** *will worship and then* **we** *will come back to you."*

From what we know from Scripture, Abraham knew exactly what he was saying. He expected that he and Isaac would return to the servants.

Hebrews gives an insight in here. By this time Abraham had come to know that God could be trusted; that he is always, always true to his word. God had promised that through Isaac his offspring would arise. Abraham knows that Isaac can die and remain dead. The writer to the Hebrews tells us that Abraham believed that even if he sacrificed his son, God would raise him from the dead (Heb 11).

Isaac's question and Abraham's response

Isaac is probably in his late teens maybe even older. There is a word for 'child' and one for 'young man'. The word in this passage is definitely 'young man'. In other words Isaac was strong enough to overcome his elderly father. Now Isaac asks the question. He is carrying the wood; his father has the fire in an earthenware vessel but no burnt offering. So he asks the question.

> Abraham took the wood for the burnt offering and placed it on his son Isaac, and he himself carried the fire and the knife. As the two of them went on together, ⁷ Isaac spoke up and said to his father Abraham, "Father?"
> "Yes, my son?" Abraham replied.
> "The fire and wood are here," Isaac said, "but where is the lamb for the burnt offering?"
> ⁸ Abraham answered, "God himself will provide the lamb for the burnt offering, my son." And the two of them went on together.

אֱלֹהִים יִרְאֶה־לּוֹ הַשֶּׂה לְעֹלָה

Abraham's answer is probably the most important statement in the entire passage "God himself will provide the lamb." The word for provide here is the word Yireh.

The Crucial Moment

They reach the place God had told Abraham about. The narrator slows down and deliberately records every action of Abraham. Isaac, no doubt, lays down the wood at the chosen spot. Abraham builds an altar. That must have taken a while. He then carefully lays the wood on the altar. At what point Abraham broke the fatal news to Isaac, we do not know.

Finally, Abraham binds his son Isaac and lays him on the altar, on top of the wood, and reaches out his hand and takes the sharp knife. He does not hesitate. He is going through with it! Once he has slit Isaac's jugular, he will set the wood alight. . Probably Isaac's reaction is as amazing as Abraham's.

At that very moment a voice rings out:
> *"Abraham! Abraham!"*
> *"Here I am," he replied.*
> *"Do not lay a hand on the boy," he said. "Do not do anything to him. Now I know that you fear God, because you have not withheld from me your son, your only son"* (Gen. 22:11-12).

What a moment that must have been for Abraham--*and for Isaac!* "Abraham looked up and there in the thicket he saw a ram caught by its horns. He went over took the ram and sacrificed it as a burnt offering instead of his son. We can imagine the two of them standing side by side, perhaps arm in arm as they watch the smoke ascend form the burnt offering. Talk about a poignant moment! **So Abraham called the name of that place, *Yahweh Yireh*** ("Jehovah Jireh")--"The LORD will Provide." And to this day it is said, 'On the mountain of the LORD it will be provided'" (Gen. 22:13-14*).*

THE THEME IS ONE THAT RUNS FROM GENESIS TO REVELATION.

God did not become *Yahweh Yireh* at this moment. He has always been the God who provides. And he does so in so many ways. But let me place the accent where Scripture places it.

I would like to make the point here. You know the word 'provision'. We don't always understand these words, the etymology of the word. Provision comes from two Latin words, 'pro' – before and 'vision' - to see – to see beforehand. The root of the word 'to provide' in Hebrew is 'to see'. When going on a picnic, you take provisions with you. You know beforehand what is needed. In the story we have a God is who looks ahead and provides beforehand. God did not become Yahweh Yireh at this moment. He always was.

The garments
In the first 3 chapters of Genesis we have very simple narration but very profound theology. When mankind fell God came looking for Adam and Eve. No sooner had God pronounced judgment on them than he provided for their immediate need: *"The LORD God made garments of skin for Adam and his wife and clothed them"* (Gen. 3:21). Again and again we see God anticipating needs and providing for them ("Provision").

And God set in motion a plan to provide for the greatest of all human needs.

The sacrificial system
*"For the life of a creature is in the blood, and **I have given it to you** to make atonement for yourselves on the altar; it is the blood that makes atonement for one's life."* (Lev 17:11)

The system points forward to God's ultimate provision
We all, like sheep, have gone astray,
each of us has turned to our own way;
and the Lord has laid on him
the iniquity of us all.
⁷ He was oppressed and afflicted,
yet he did not open his mouth;
he was led like a lamb to the slaughter,
and as a sheep before its shearers is silent,
so he did not open his mouth. (Isa 53:6-7)

Behold the Lamb
Think of John the Baptist. Everyone is excited. He is preaching, a prophetic voice after 400 years. They ask him, "Are you the Messiah?" He answers that he is not and then:
> *"The next day John saw Jesus coming toward him and said, "Look the Lamb of God who takes away the sin of the world"*

Abraham's words were truer than he realised: "God himself will provide a lamb".

Before the creation of the world
> *"For you know that it was not with perishable things such as silver or gold that you were redeemed from the empty way of life handed down to you from your ancestors, [19] but with the precious blood of Christ, a lamb without blemish or defect. [20] He was chosen before the creation of the world, but was revealed in these last times for your sake* (1 Pet 1:18-19).

That is provision, seeing ahead and providing.

Now there are wonderful assurances that God will provide our needs.

I think of that great statement in 2 Corinthians 9: *"God is able to make all grace abound to you, so that in all things at all times, having all that you need you will abound in every good work. . . . You will be made rich in every way so that you can be generous on every occasion* (2 Cor. 9:8, 11).

Paul assures the Philippians in categorical terms: *"My God will meet all your needs according to his glorious riches **in Christ Jesus**"* (Phil 4:19).

But that's the key – "in Christ Jesus". Let's not sell ourselves short by focussing on this or that provision. When we say *Yahweh Yireh*, we are thinking of his ultimate gift. And that gift cost him everything he had. That's why Paul can say: *"He who did not spare his own Son, but gave him up for us all—how will he not also, along with him, graciously give us all things?* (Rom 8:32)

CONCLUSION

God, himself, has gone to such incredible lengths. There was no one to say to God, "Don't harm your son.' The son has voluntarily come for that very reason. He has made abundant provision for our greatest need. He invites you to trust him. Look at what God has done for you.

Does this not inspire your heart? God has provided and now I can trust him.

יְהוָה נִסִּי

Yahweh Nissi: **The LORD my Banner**

Reading: Exodus 17:8-16

In July I had the privilege of spending a week at a summer school in Oxford. One of the highlights was a visit to "the Kilns," the home occupied by the Oxford don and Cambridge professor, C. S. Lewis. For years, Lewis has been one of my favourite authors. We had an excellent guide and I felt I knew Lewis, *the man*, better as a result of the visit.

The first of Lewis' books that I read was a book called **The Screwtape Letters**. Lewis uses his vivid imagination to give us what is purportedly correspondence between a senior demon, Screwtape and a junior demon, his protégé, Wormwood.

It is a clever portrayal. By using this subversive approach, Lewis is able to alert us to some of the wiles of the devil. Allow me to give you a sample from one of the letters.

> My dear Wormwood,
> I wonder you should ask me whether it is essential to keep the patient in ignorance of your own existence. . . . Our policy, for the moment, is to conceal ourselves. . . . I do not think you will have much difficulty in keeping the patient in the dark. The fact that devils are predominantly *comic* figures in the modern imagination will help you. If any faint suspicion of your existence begins to arise in his mind, suggest to him a picture of something in red tights, and persuade him that since he cannot

believe in *that* (it is an old textbook method of confusing them) he therefore cannot believe in *you*.[14]

Lewis is hardly the sort of man to adopt a sensationalist approach. He would not be into what some call "spiritual warfare," blaming everything bad on direct demonic influence, binding demons, and revelling in the idea of spiritual combat. But he was convinced in the existence of real, malevolent, intelligent, spiritual beings, who are responsible for much of the evil in the world.

And so am I. In fact, according to Scripture, we are involved in a cosmic battle. This is not a matter of choice. We cannot say, "We will leave that to those who are into that kind of stuff and we'll get on with a more down-to-earth Christian life."

The teaching of the New Testament on this subject is unambiguous. I shall mention just two passages. Paul tells us to

> "Be strong in the Lord and in his mighty power. (He reminds us that) our struggle is not against flesh and blood, but against the rulers, against the authorities, against the powers of this dark world and against the spiritual forces of evil in the heavenly realms. And he makes it clear that we will only be able to stand if we clothe ourselves with the armour of God." (Eph. 6:10-12).

He knew he was in a battle with an uncompromising enemy but he knew that God is all we could ever need for victory:

> "Though we live in the world, we do not wage war as the world does. The weapons we fight with are not the weapons of the world. On the contrary, they have divine power to demolish

---

[14] *The Screwtape Letters,* C.S. Lewis, 1942

strongholds. We demolish arguments and every pretension that sets itself up against the knowledge of God, and we take captive every thought to make it obedient to Christ"
(2 Cor 10:3 - 5).

So I have bad news and good news this morning. The bad news is that the battle is unavoidable. The good news is that God has given us everything we could possibly need to be victorious in this battle.

So let's try to put see the matter in biblical perspective as we look at the passage before us today.

THE AMALEKITES ATTACK

The Israelites have left Egypt and are travelling through the Sinai Peninsula. They are on their way to Mount Sinai and ultimately to Canaan. They have absolutely no intention of attacking anyone en route to the Promised Land.

Imagine that you are a spectator perched on a hill in the Sinai Peninsula. You are able to observe this huge company making its way through the desert. You notice that some of the more vulnerable travellers are lagging behind. Evening is about to fall. And then you see the Amalekites sneak up and attack those at the rear and mow them down mercilessly. The message gets through to Moses and he summons Joshua and instructs him to marshal a make-shift army to fight the Amalekites on the following day.

As you watch the battle, you are amazed at the fluctuating fortunes of the Israelites. At times they drive back the Amalekites with relative ease. Then the tide turns and the Amalekites are successful. Then the Israelites have the upper hand again. And so the fortunes fluctuate.

You then notice that three men are on top of the opposite hill. The central figure is Moses and with him are Aaron and Hur. Moses' hands are raised to heaven as he lifts the staff, which had served as a sign of God's presence in Egypt and at the Red Sea. The Israelites outmatch the Amalekites. Moses' hands tire and he lowers them. But as he does so the tide turns again. This pattern continues. Whenever his hands are raised the Israelites gain the ascendency, but whenever they are lowered the Amalekites are in control.

You then see Aaron and Hur pushing a large stone so that Moses can be seated on it. They stand on either side of him and hold his hands up for several hours. Joshua wins the battle and the Amalekites are forced to flee.

There is a point of major spiritual significance in the account. Moses built an altar and called it ***Yahweh Nissi--the LORD is my Banner***. He said, "For hands were lifted up to the throne of the LORD." The altar was built and named to make one thing crystal clear: ***the LORD had granted victory***. It was obvious that Joshua's army was able to gain the upper hand only when Moses' hands were lifted up to the throne of God.

THERE ARE FIVE REALLY IMPORTANT SPIRITUAL PRINCIPLES FOR US IN THIS PASSAGE.

The LORD himself does more than any banner could do.

Ordinarily a banner was intended to be a rallying point for an army. It represented what they are fighting for and boosted morale. Hopefully it struck fear into the enemy as well. In a sense, the sight of Moses at the top of the hill, rod in hand, and arms raised to heaven, may have been like a banner to the army. But there was more to it than that. The attack had come suddenly. There was no time for any of the customary battle preparations, one of which would possibly have been the erection of a banner. But the attack was an attack on the people of God and Moses was interceding with the LORD for his people. Instead of fighting under a banner which would provide a psychological boost, Israel was fighting under the throne of Yahweh. He is **Yahweh Nissi**—their unseen banner. What a banner is intended to do, *Yahweh*, in fact, does, and much more!

We have to be clear that the LORD and only the LORD can give us victory in this battle.

Joshua couldn't think it was his generalship that secured the victory. He knew full well that the Israelites only prevailed when Moses' hands were raised. It was not Moses' prayer, as such, (symbolized by his upraised hands) that provided the victory. Moses didn't have the strength to keep his arms raised. Aaron and Hur couldn't take too much credit. All they were doing was to help hold Moses' hands up. Only when hands were lifted up to the throne of God were the Israelites victorious. Clearly, the victory was attributable to him.

There can be no compromise here, no détente; co-existence is simply not possible.

Although our focus is upon this particular incident, we have to see it as an episode in an ongoing enmity (Deut. 25:19; 1 Sam. 15:20, 32 to 34; Esther 3:1, 8, 9). In fact, it was as though opposition to and hatred of Israel was built into the DNA of the Amalekites. They were closely related to Israel. Amalek was a descendant of Esau (Gen. 36:12).

Saul was instructed to destroy them. It is ironic that the young man who ultimately bore responsibility for Saul's death was an Amalekite (2 Sam 1:8-10). Apparently, you just could not afford to compromise with the Amalekites. There simply could be no co-existence with the Amalekites. Years later, in the days of Queen Esther, a man by the name of Haman attempted to eradicate all Jews from the Persian Empire. He was an Amalekite. To this day the passage (Ex 17:8-16) is read at the Feast of Purim, which celebrates the deliverance of the Jews in Haman's proposed holocaust.

I remember a young man who came to the Lord in exceptional circumstances attending a prayer meeting. He was full of zeal and love for everyone. So he prayed for the devil's salvation. I wish that was possible. But his opposition is entrenched and incorrigible.

Jesus urged us to take radical steps to eliminate anything that is likely to trip us up (Matt. 5:28-29). There is too much at stake here! The same principle applies today. To be a believer is to be involved in a war with an enemy who is bent on your total destruction.

There can be no greater folly than self-reliance.

We can achieve nothing that is of spiritual value in our own strength. Let me be practical here. If our objective is to get people from the community to associate with us, we can devise ways to do that. But that's not what we are after. We want them to come to faith in Jesus. Nothing better can happen for them. But we cannot bring a single person to genuine faith in Christ. Not one! That is the reason we are here. Our reason for existence is for people to be liberated from the bondage of sin, and come to know the Lord as personal Saviour. All the other things we do, important as they are, are with that end in mind.

No matter what we do, no matter how hard we try, we in our own strength and our own programmes, cannot effect the salvation on one person because there is a spiritual dynamic.

People are only genuinely saved when the Spirit of God does what none of us is able to do. That has to be a work of God. Hands have to be lifted up to the throne of God. Ultimately, we are dealing with spiritual matters, not convincing people.

Some of us are a little slow on the uptake. This is a lesson God has to teach me again and again. Let me give you one instance.

Shortly before I came to Canada, I was involved in a church move from one location to another. It involved the acquisition of several large properties and the consolidation of those properties. Then we had to advertise to the area in order to get permission to build. We had taken great care to make sure that the building of a large church complex would not affect the community negatively. We sent out notifications to the people of the plans. I expected there would be a bit of opposition, there always is. The opposition was unbelievable. It was as though you had stirred up a hornet's nest. Such lies were told, and then we discovered that there were all sorts of shenanigans going on and probably payments that we knew nothing about. We had rich, determined, influential opponents. So, one of the things I had to do was write a letter to the 300 odd people who had lodged personal objections. I tried to gently and politely explain and debunk some of the lies that were told. Then I inserted a paragraph to tell them in no uncertain terms that we would take this matter to the highest tribunal in the land if need be. I assured them that by no stretch of the imagination, could they think that they could intimidate us – not quite in those words. I thought they needed to know that we were not going to buckle under pressure.

A man who is experienced in these matters, saw the letter and commented that it was a good letter but that paragraph didn't sound like me. I think he was wrong and that it was just like me. The letter had already been sent. As I pondered what he said, I realise that I had taken the law into my own hands.

We got a tribunal date we called a prayer meeting. We had been told by others that we never had a chance. On the way to the prayer meeting, I received a message that the tribunal had been postponed. How was I to tell the people who had come to pray that the tribunal the next day had been postponed? I told the gathering but God had done something in the hearts of those people and my own heart. You should have heard those prayers. There was such an atmosphere of belief and confidence and positive sense that God was in control. We had a tribunal date 10 days later.

The tribunal members and the church representatives had to first visit the site. The chair of the tribunal was known to be a Jewish Communist. The main opponents were also there. The latter so disgraced themselves behaving in a childish manner although they were intelligent people. I realised that something was happening. At the tribunal venue, the case was presented, there was almost a sense of God's presence – because the battles is not ours. The battle is the Lord's.

Something had happened. We received the required permission. An article appeared in the newspaper in which the chair of the tribunal wrote very disparagingly about those who had opposed the scheme. Within a relatively short space of time many of those who had signed to oppose the development, were using our facility and it had become a community centre. But I had had to learn that the battle was not mine, the silly paragraph should never have occurred, the battle is the Lord's not mine. It is his work and only he can do it.

This is a battle in which victory is guaranteed.
When we say *Yahweh Nissi*, we are declaring a simple principle that is exemplified again and again in Scripture. Think of young David heading out with his shepherd's sling and pouch, a sling and five stones to face the monster Goliath who was armed to the teeth. Hear what he says to Goliath: "All those gathered here will know that it is not by sword or spear that the Lord saves; for *the battle is the Lord's*, and he will give all of you into our hands" (1 Sam 17:47).

To my mind, the clearest statement of this principle is found in the prayer of King Jehoshaphat. The king received news that a vast army was marching against Jerusalem. He proclaimed a fast. Then he stood up in the temple of the LORD and prayed. Listen to how he commences his prayer:

> "O LORD, God of our ancestors, are you not the God who is in heaven? You rule over all the kingdoms of the nations. Power and might are in your hand, and no one can withstand you." (2 Chron 20:6)

And listen to how he concludes it:

> "Our God, will you not judge them? For we have no power to face this vast army that is attacking us. We do not know what to do, but our eyes are on you." (2 Chron 20:12)

In response, the Spirit of the LORD came on the prophet Jahaziel and he said,

> "Listen, King Jehoshaphat and all who live in Judah and Jerusalem! This is what the Lord says to you: 'Do not be afraid or discouraged because of this vast army. For the battle is not yours, but God's'" (2 Chron 20:6, 12, 15).

Through Isaiah, the LORD assures us:

> 'No weapon forged against you will prevail,
> and you will refute every tongue that accuses you.
> This is the heritage of the servants of the LORD,
> And this is the vindication from me,' declares the LORD
> (Isa. 54:17).

Conclusion

It seems so simple. There is a battle that we cannot win without the LORD and that we cannot lose with the LORD. But hands have to be lifted to the throne of God. I am encouraged that there are many people in our church who take prayer very seriously indeed. But I wonder if this is still not our greatest need.

May I remind you that God is still on the throne.

Prayer of Jehoshaphat: "Lord, the God of our ancestors, are you not the God who is in heaven? You rule over all the kingdoms of the nations. Power and might are in your hand, and no one can withstand you. . . We have no power to face this vast army that is attacking us. We do not know what to do, **but our eyes are on you.**"
(2 Chron 20:6, 12)

יְהוָה רֹפְאֶךָ

Yahweh Rophecha: The LORD Who Heals You

Readings: Exodus 15:22-27; James 5:14

Is physical healing available to us today? If so, should we not be seeing miracles of healing such as we read about in the Bible: the blind seeing, the lame walking the deaf hearing, and here and there the dead being raised to life? What about those massive, high-powered and much-controverted healing meetings? Yes, in some cases, there is sensationalism and no doubt there is dishonesty and showmanship but let's not decide the matter on the basis of our aversion to this or that religious celebrity.

Some of us may want these questions answered because we are puzzled or even curious. But my main concern is pastoral, not polemic. These questions may be of some academic interest, but what happens if your child or grandchild is diagnosed with leukaemia? What happens if, after years of good health, you are told that you have a terminal illness that will take your life in a matter of months? What do you do then? Do you accept the inevitability of it all or do you seek healing from the Lord? Do you ask the church to pray or do you attend the meeting of someone who is said to have a gift of healing? These pressing questions are no longer academic. To attempt to answer them, we must start at the beginning.

GOD DESCRIBES HIMSELF AS *YAHWEH ROPHECHA*: THE LORD WHO HEALS YOU.

The Incident

The circumstances under which the LORD revealed himself as *Yahweh Rophecha* are highly significant. The Israelites had just passed through the Red Sea. Behind them were some of the most amazing events in history. They had experienced slavery and oppression, but they had seen God deliver them through a series of devastating plagues. The worst of these plagues were the epidemics that struck the people. The festering boils must have caused real misery. The final plague resulted in the death of the firstborn throughout the land.

After the miraculous passage through the Red Sea, there was a great celebration. Moses and the Israelites danced and sang a song of praise to the LORD (Ex. 15:1-2, 11-13). There was excitement and jubilation when Miriam led the women, with tambourines in hand, as they danced for joy (Ex. 15:21).

Nothing is more likely to take the song out of one's heart than three days travel in the hot and arid region of the Sinai Peninsula. Their water bottles, filled before they left Egypt, were now empty. They were tired. They had never travelled in the region and there was no water in sight. There were a lot of them. The anxiety level must have risen towards the end of the second day. By the third day they would have begun to panic. But they controlled themselves and travelled on.

Then they came across an oasis. Water at last! When you are that thirsty you don't dilly-dally. I'm sure that those at the front of the company dashed to the water's edge and began to gulp down the water. Can you imagine the gasps of disappointment when they realised that they had discovered brackish water, bitter to the taste and quite undrinkable? The angry complaints began to flow. They directed their anger at Moses asking, "What are we to drink?" Moses cried out to the LORD. And the LORD showed him a piece of wood. He threw it into the water and it immediately became fresh. This was probably the best water they had ever tasted.

The Declaration
Clearly this was an enacted parable. This was not a bit of magic. There was nothing in the wood that made the water sweet. The message was clear. God could have ensured that the water was fresh before they arrived. The piece of wood did not change the water's composition. But God chose to "heal" the waters and in so doing he was saying: *"I am not just your Saviour and Deliverer from bondage; I am your Provider and Healer. You needed me to get you out of Egypt and I proved faithful. You need me to sustain you on your journey, and I will remain faithful."* Then the LORD made a decree for them:

> If you will listen carefully to the voice of the LORD your God and do what is right in his eyes, if you pay attention to his commands and keep all his decrees, I will not bring on you any of the diseases I brought on the Egyptians, for I am *Yahweh Rophecha* (the LORD who heals you). (Ex 15:26)

God demonstrated that he was true to his word. At the end of Israel's period of wandering in the Wilderness, Moses was able to say:

> Remember how the LORD your God led you all the way in the desert to humble you and to test you in order to know what was in your heart, whether or not you would keep his commands. . . . Your clothes did not wear out and your feet did not swell during these forty years (Deut. 8:2, 4).

The Meaning
We have to be careful not to read into this passage what is not there. Certainly the LORD was saying, *"I am not just your Saviour and Deliverer from bondage; I am your Provider and Healer. You needed me to get you out of Egypt and I proved faithful. You need me to sustain you on your journey, and I will remain faithful."*

THIS IS, BY NO MEANS A PERIPHERAL SUBJECT: HEALING IS AT THE HEART OF SCRIPTURE.

The Sweep of Scripture
Whenever we seek to understand God's mind on a subject like this (or on any subject for that matter), we need to take the teaching of the whole sweep of Scripture into account. It does not help to look at a passage or two, form a premature opinion and then discard or argue away other passages. So let me make a few observations about the teaching of scripture as a whole.

The Old Testament
We see a number of instances of healing in the Old Testament, people like Miriam, Naaman, and Hezekiah.

The New Testament
We know that miracles of healing played an important part in the ministry of Jesus, causing people to gasp in amazement, declaring, "We have never seen anything like this!" Matthew informs us that "Jesus went throughout Galilee, teaching in their synagogues, preaching the good news of the kingdom, and healing every disease and sickness among the people" (Matt 4:23). Healing was a major feature of his ministry, not just an authentication of his message but part of who he was and what he had come to do.

We then notice that healing was a major component of the ministry of the apostles. We can think of the lame man at the gate of the temple whose healing caused a huge stir. We are told that the apostles performed many miraculous signs and wonders among the people. When Paul was at Ephesus, Dr. Luke tells us that God did extraordinary miracles through him (Acts 19:11). So physical healing was very much part of the ministry of the early church.

When it came to believers in the church, James asks, "Is any one of you sick. Let them call the elders of the church to pray over them and anoint them with oil in the name of the Lord. And the prayer offered in faith will make them well; the Lord will raise them up. If they have sinned, they will be forgiven" (Jas 5:13-15).

Balance
How important it is that we adopt a balanced approach to this subject. As always, Scripture is balanced. But unfortunately some people come to premature conclusions. So I shall briefly mention **four matters** that we need to take into account.

1. The Bible views healing in holistic terms. Sadly, "brokenness" is part of the human condition. And the word for healing in the Old Testament does not only refer to physical healing. It is also used of psychological and spiritual healing. So we read in Psalm 147:3 that *the LORD heals the broken-hearted and binds up their wounds*. David cries out, *"O LORD, have mercy on me; heal me, for I have sinned against you"* (Psa 41:4). The LORD says through the prophet Hosea, *"I will heal their waywardness and love them freely, for my anger has turned away from them"* (Hos 14:4). **The essential thought in healing is restoration to a state of wholeness and normality.** And this can be spiritual or mental or physical well-being. In fact, these aspects of God's healing are often much more closely related that we realise.

2. We live in the interim between the "already" and the "not yet." From the time we come to know the Lord, a healing process begins. But it is not complete until we see the Lord. This means that some of us will battle with physical illness. Very few can say that they are in absolute perfect health. Have you been to the dentist recently? Do you wear spectacles?

3. We do come across some sick Christians in the New Testament. Paul tells the Philippians that his fellow-worker, Epaphroditus, was ill and almost died, but God had mercy on him (Phil 2:27). He refers to his own health problem and acknowledged that God used it for good. He is explicit when he writes to the Galatians: "As you know, it was because of an illness that I first preached the gospel to you. Even though my illness was a trial to you, you did not treat me with contempt and scorn" (Gal 4:13-14). He mentions to Timothy that he had to leave Trophimus sick in Miletus (2Tim 4:20). There are some sick Christians and we mustn't jump to conclusions as to why they are not healed.

4. Not too far beneath the surface is the question of whether matters like physical healing were reserved for New Testament days. There are people we call cessationists who believe that the miracles are confined to the New Testament. Others believe that we should be seeing dramatic miracles of healing and anything short of that is a failure. John Stott acknowledges this very principle that God can do anything at any time but argues that it is true that supernatural often cluster around events of revelation in history. God is not obliged to do the same thing in the same way. Yes, there have been wonderful revivals in church history where there was very little physical healing but God Spirit was so powerfully at work in awakenings in the United States, the Welsh Revival, with the accent not necessarily on physical healing but great things happened. God remains sovereign at all times.

So what are we to do as a church and what should you do if you discover that you need physical healing?

HERE IS WHAT I SUGGEST YOU DO IF YOU ARE IN NEED OF HEALING.

If you have been led to believe that every Christian has the right to perfect health, I need to disabuse you. There are a number of problems with this approach. First, it says more than Scripture does. Second, it has some unfortunate effects. Its proponents say that if you are sick, it is either because you have sinned or because you have no faith. Some who hold the same position do so largely because they feel that it enables us to be positive and to exercise faith. If God has promised our healing and provided for it, then we can boldly claim it. They contend that it is not possible to exercise faith if we can't be absolutely sure that we will be healed. The "name-it-and-claim-it" approach is unbiblical and unhelpful.

At the other extreme is the view that, to all intents and purposes, relegates healing to the past. In reality, we don't really expect God to heal us. We say, "Thy will be done," but there is such a note of resignation about it, that we practically cancel our prayer. We may call this resignation.

The third approach is to recognize that God is *Yahweh Rophecha* and to come to *him* in faith. It means that we cast ourselves upon him. We don't have to accept that it is always his will to heal every person in order to come to him. The problem with the first approach is that it takes God out of the equation and rests in a formula. We are dealing with the healing and not the Healer.

I remember hearing the true story of a couple whose child became terminally ill. His life was in the balance and they were understandably desperate. They prayed earnestly and many of their Christian friends joined them. They begged like the widow who would give the unjust judge no rest until he heeded her request. But the condition of their little son was unchanged. Eventually they could take it no more. So they "gave him" to the Lord, not in a spirit of passive resignation but in the spirit of active faith. "Lord, you gave him to us and we give him back to you. He is yours. If you want to take him to be with you, that is your prerogative. We would like him to be with us but we surrender him to you. He's yours, Lord." A deep peace settled over them. And from that moment there was a change in his condition. He was healed!

Some have called this **"the prayer of relinquishment."** There is a world of difference between relinquishment and resignation. **Resignation gives up and relinquishment gives over!** Resignation is a fatalistic "whatever-will-be-will-be." Relinquishment is trusting God and bowing before his sovereign grace.

To be true there have been other cases of surrender in which healing has not taken place. But such has been the sense of peace that there was no doubt that the Great Physician was present. At times one has almost felt that he was saying a gentle "No" to the request for healing but a certain "Yes" to us all as pilgrims and strangers whose citizenship is in heaven. Paul placed all that happens to us in this life in perspective when he said,

We eagerly await a Saviour from there, the Lord Jesus Christ, who, by the power that enables him to bring everything under his control, will transform our lowly bodies so that they will be like his glorious body (Phil. 3:20-21; cf. Heb. 11:13- 16; I Pet. 2:11-12).

Conclusion

So, what should we do? A responsible attitude is to certainly trust the Lord but that doesn't mean we stop taking our medication. As a church we should pray for anyone who asks.

And what should you do?

At any time we can come to the Lord because he cares and he still heals today. I cannot tell you that everyone who comes received healing but I can tell you that those who come receive wonderful peace which passes all understanding.

Pray for health workers.

Pray for healing.

יְהוָה שָׁלוֹם

Yahweh Shalom: The LORD our Peace

Readings: Judges 6:11-24; Ephesians 2:14-18

On 30th September 1938, Neville Chamberlain, then the prime minister of Great Britain, made a speech from Number 10 Downing Street. For some time he had followed a policy of appeasement toward Hitler and Mussolini. Chamberlain had just returned from a meeting with Adolf Hitler in Munich. He described his diplomatic victory with characteristic modesty:

> This is the second time in our history that there has come back from Germany to Downing Street peace with honour. I believe it is peace for our time.

With his usual candour, Winston Churchill described Chamberlain's European escapade as "a total, unmitigated defeat." Soon Britain was at war and, not long after, Chamberlain was out of office. Unfortunately, in this fallen world of ours, lasting peace seems elusive. Regional conflicts abound, often accompanied by atrocities. And we don't have to be alarmist to recognise that one of these can escalate into a large-scale war. And some national leaders are not renowned for their moderation and a sense of responsibility.

But let's bring this closer to home. At a personal and domestic level, we experience tension. You may not get along with your boss, a particular neighbour, your parents, your children, your siblings, or your spouse. You may not even get along with yourself! And one or more of these fractured relationships may be causing you a great deal of grief.

Of course, peace is an elastic term. A "peace" of sorts can be imposed. Repression can put a lid on discord. When our children were small, we sometimes travelled 1 500 kilometres on holiday. As you may have experienced, it is difficult for two bored siblings to co-exist in peace for hour after hour. When they had run out of games, the niggling would start. Before too long, they would be going at it. They had a whole back seat but they became extremely territorial. Accusations and protestations of innocence, jabbing elbows and even the odd foot! And children figure out when they can get away with things. They knew we were in the front seat and my hands were on the steering wheel. On one occasion, when the niggling started, I jammed on the brakes, pulled over to the side of the road, and made a little speech. The choice was simple. I was not going to have strife in the car. If their niggling persisted, they could get out and walk the rest of the way. Apparently, they believed me and there was a long period of harmony. But the devil finds work for idle hands. So the slightly muted niggling would start up again. All I had to do was to apply the brakes and pull over to the side and there was peace, perfect peace. Actually, no! There was silence. Threats and brute force can put a lid on conflict. But that does not necessarily mean there is peace. Peace imposed by force is not true peace.

There is also the "peace" that comes from placation and compromise. We may enjoy a temporary "peace" that purposely ignores issues of justice. The "peace" that flows from placation is usually short-lived and often counterproductive. It is more like a truce but it ignores the root causes of the problem.

This morning we are going to be looking at the real thing—at genuine peace. And we are going to be considering the fact that God is described repeatedly in Scripture as the God of peace. In particular, we are going to encounter God as *Yahweh Shalom*, the LORD is peace. That's a name that was given to the altar Gideon built to commemorate the revelation of God's character to him.

But first, let me make a point that is crucial to all we shall consider today. In this fallen world genuine peace often comes at a huge price. *The pathway to peace inevitably runs through the conflict zone of adversity and strife.*

We'll start with our passage and then expand our consideration to the theme as it occurs throughout Scripture.

PEACE AT A PRICE.

The Midianite Menace

When the Israelites entered the land of Canaan, God promised to bless them abundantly. If, however, they disobeyed him, they were destined to suffer at the hands of their enemies. And it is abundantly clear from the first two chapters of the Book of Judges that they did disobey him. As a result of their disobedience, the Israelites had to face stout resistance from within their borders and devastating incursions from without. The situation was dreadful. For seven years the Midianites, together with the Amalekites and other Eastern peoples oppressed them. They would wait for the Israelites to plant their crops and then come in their hoards and vindictively ruin the crops. There were so many of them and they were so destructive that the Midianite army resembled a swarm of locusts. They did not spare a living thing, neither sheep, nor cattle, nor donkeys. They ravaged the land and impoverished the Israelites.

The Course of Least Resistance

But the Israelites found a way to keep the "peace". They prepared shelters for themselves in the mountain clefts, caves and strongholds. When the Midianites invaded the land, the Israelites went into hiding. This would go on year after year until the Israelites were so impoverished that they cried out to the LORD in desperation. Like the rest of his compatriots, young Gideon was taking the course of least resistance. He was threshing wheat in a winepress to keep it from the Midianites.

The Stranger
One day a Stranger came and sat down under a nearby oak tree which belonged to Joash, Gideon's father. He greeted Gideon with the words, "The LORD is with you, mighty warrior." That designation took Gideon by surprise. He objected. "Sir, if the LORD is with us, why has all this happened to us?" But the Stranger replied, "Go in the strength you have and save Israel out of Midian's hand. Am I not sending you?" "But Lord," Gideon asked, "how can I save Israel?[15] My clan is the weakest in Manasseh, and I am the least in my family." The LORD answered, "I will be with you, and you will strike down all the Midianites together."

By this time Gideon must have wondered just who it was that was speaking to him. He addressed the Stranger as Adoni (v. 13; Adonai, v. 15), which can mean "Lord" or just "Sir." The Stranger's instruction seemed so authoritative. But the ever-cautious Gideon did not want to jump to conclusions. So he asked the Stranger to wait while he prepared a meal. Showing such hospitality to visitors was customary courtesy in the east. But interestingly, the word used by Gideon to describe the meal was a word that can be used to describe a "meat offering". He was not sure of the identity of the Stranger. If the Stranger treated the offering as a normal meal, then he was an

---

[15]Initially (v. 13) Gideon uses the term *Adoni* (a singular noun with a possessive pronominal suffix) meaning lord or sir, a term of respect usually used to refer to an esteemed man. Then, in v. 15, he addresses the Stranger as Adonai (the plural form of the noun with a possessive pronominal suffix). In Scripture, when the term *Adonai* (in the plural) is used, it almost always refers to God.

important human visitor. If he accepted it as an offering, then something extraordinary was happening.

The Meal/Offering
So Gideon prepared the meal and brought it out to the Stranger under the oak tree. The Stranger asked him to place the food on the rock and to pour out the broth. Then with the tip of the staff that was in his hand, the Stranger touched the meat and the unleavened bread. Fire flared from the rock, consuming the meat and the bread. And, in an instant, the Stranger disappeared.

Shalom
Gideon realized that it was "the angel of the LORD". He cried out, "Ah Sovereign LORD (*Adonai Yahweh*)! I have seen the Angel of the LORD face to face!" Realizing that he had been conversing with God, he expected to die (see Ex 33:20). Immediately the LORD reassured him: "Peace (Shalom)! Do not be afraid. You are not going to die." As we examine the passage, and particularly the names used to describe Gideon's visitor, it is clear that this was a "theophany", an appearance of the Lord in angelic form. When we read of "the Angel of the LORD" the reference is not just to one angel among many; it is not even to a special angelic messenger. This is God assuming angelic appearance long before he took on our humanity in the incarnation. The same person is described here as, "the angel of the LORD (*Yahweh*)", "LORD (*Yahweh*)", "Lord (*Adonai*)", "the angel of God (*Elohim*)" and "Sovereign LORD (*Adonai Yahweh*)".

The Altar
In response to all that had happened, Gideon built an altar to the LORD and called it *Yahweh Shalom*—"The LORD is Peace". This was no doubt because of the LORD's first word to him after he discovered that he had seen the Angel of the LORD: "*Shalom*--Peace!" Realizing that God had graciously spared his life, Gideon wished to

commemorate the revelation that the LORD is *Yahweh Shalom*, the God of Peace. But there is more to the use of this name than the fact that Gideon's life was spared. The one who revealed himself as *Yahweh Shalom* was about to bring peace to his people by delivering them from Midianite oppression.

The Israelites may have thought that their evasive action had afforded them a measure of peace. But they had settled for a "peace" with disgrace, a "peace" that, in the long run, cost them so dearly that almost anything was preferable to their predicament. Now Yahweh Shalom is about to give them "peace with honour".

The Pathway to Peace
As we saw, the pathway to peace inevitably runs through the conflict zone of adversity and strife. And the route to this peace was not going to be easy. In this fallen world it never is. First there has to be trouble. Gideon must risk his life. He must tear down his own father's altar to Baal and cut down the Asherah pole beside it. He must then build an altar to the LORD and sacrifice a mature bull from his father's herd on it, using the wood of the Asherah pole as firewood for the burnt offering. With the help of ten of his servants, Gideon waited for nightfall and did as the LORD had commanded him. The next morning the town woke up to find, to its horror, that Baal's altar had been demolished, the Asherah pole cut down and a bull sacrificed on the newly built altar. They were so incensed that they wanted to kill the culprit. Gideon's father came to his son's defence and Gideon was nicknamed "Jerub-Baal", meaning "Let Baal contend." In other words, it was accepted that Gideon had antagonized not just his fellow citizens but Baal himself and had incurred the wrath of the Canaanite god.

The human condition is such that a cheap peace is no peace at all. Real peace involves the righting of wrongs. Lasting peace is only possible where justice exists. Genuine peace must address the fundamentals of our condition. Such peace, as we shall see, is extremely costly.

Peace through Conflict
The story of Gideon is fairly well known from this point on. When next the Midianites and their allies crossed over the Jordan River to devastate the land, the Spirit of the LORD came upon Gideon and he blew a trumpet, summoning the members of his clan to follow him. Messengers were sent throughout the tribe of Manasseh, calling them to arms. Three of the other northern tribes were also summoned people from the tribes of Asher, Zebulun and Naphtali.

Once again, Gideon sought confirmation, this time by means of his fleece. He asked that his fleece be sopping wet in the morning and the ground around it bone dry. Ruling out any chance of coincidence, he asked that on the second night the fleece be bone dry and the ground around it saturated. Then there were the troop reductions. First of all 22 000 were allowed to leave because they were terrified. Only 10 000 remained. But another test was required, a test which only 300 passed. It needed to be abundantly clear that God had given the Israelites victory so that they would not arrogate to themselves the credit for the conquest. It was a remarkable victory indeed. The main weapons used were trumpets and torches. The invading army was thrown into confusion, attacking one another and soundly defeated. Their power to terrorise the Israelites was broken. *Yahweh Shalom*--The LORD is Peace had restored peace to his people. It was a peace that came not through appeasement but through confrontation. For there to be real peace the issue had to be faced, not avoided. Real peace can only come when the root causes are dealt with.

THE HUGE PRICE OF ULTIMATE PEACE.

We move from an episode in which a temporary peace came because the underlying issue was dealt with to the larger issue of God's dealing with man and the bigger story that takes place in Scripture.

The Birth of Disharmony
To place this matter of peace in perspective, we need to go right back to the point at which our peace was shattered. The picture painted for us in Genesis 1 and 2 is one of harmony and well-being and tranquillity. But with the fall, strife and disharmony entered. Adam feels ashamed and hides. When God asks him what he has done, he blames Eve and has the audacity to imply that God was partly to blame for his disobedience: "The woman *you* put here with me - she gave me some fruit from the tree and I ate it" (Gen. 3:12).

Immediate Results
Look at the immediate results of human transgression. Mankind is ill-at-ease in God's presence. Adam and Eve start doing stupid things in relation to God, like assuming that he could hide from the all-seeing One. The first marital row takes place. In the very next chapter we see how the disharmony introduced at the fall results in murder as Cain rises up and kills his own brother.

Not Until the End
Not until we come to the end of Scripture do we see universal harmony. The picture we are given in the last two chapters of the Bible is one of perfect peace. No war, no hostility, no tension, no murderers or rapists, no idolaters, no liars, no fortune-tellers, nothing impure; only joy and harmony, abundance and the unhindered enjoyment of one another's company. Peace at last!

The Prince of Peace

In between these two events the subject is developed. There is the wonderful prophecy in Isaiah 9:5-7. We are so familiar with the words of verse 6 that we tend to forget that universal peace is tied to the one described as *Sar Shalom* (the Prince of Peace):

> Of the increase of his government
> and peace there will be no end.
> He will reign on David's throne
> and over his kingdom,
> establishing and upholding it
> with righteousness and justice
> from that time on and for ever.
> The zeal of the LORD Almighty
> will accomplish this (Isa. 9:7).

Beginning to End of Jesus' Ministry

Jesus entered this world of strife. He was peace personified. When he was born the angel announced, "Glory to God in the highest and on earth peace to those on whom his favour rests" (Luke 2:14). We hear him telling people whom he healed, *"Go in peace"* (Luke 7:50; 8:48). We see him rebuking the wind and saying: "Peace, be still!" And there was a great calm (Mark 4:30). To his disciples he says, "Peace I leave with you; my peace I give to you. I do not give to you as the world gives. Do not let your hearts be troubled and do not be afraid" (John 14:27). The first words he spoke to his disciples when he appeared to them after his resurrection were: "Peace be with you" (Luke 24:36).

But the Prince of Peace was often at the centre of controversy. He said to his disciples: "Do not suppose I have come to bring peace on earth. I did not come to bring peace but a sword" (Matt. 10:34). He explained that, in the process of bringing peace to this wayward world, there would be division and persecution, pain and strife.

Taking his stand on God's Word, he found himself at odds with the religious and political establishments. John explains that "light has come into the world, but people loved darkness instead of light because their deeds were evil" (John 3:19).

But his ultimate mission was the reconciliation of God and mankind (2 Cor 5:18-21). And for this to occur, he had to fight the ultimate battle. Nothing less would do. Unless the forces of evil were overcome there could be no lasting peace. It was through his death that he destroyed him who had the power of death, that is the devil (Heb 2:14; cf. Col 2:15).

PERSONAL PEACE NOW; UNIVERSAL PEACE LATER.

There is so very much that can be said about peace but I shall confine myself to four key areas this morning.

First, let me return to the important principle that I enunciated earlier: **the road to peace is often a road of conflict and strife**. Peace comes at a huge price. In this fallen world, the pathway to peace inevitably runs through the conflict zone of adversity and strife. Jesus said, "Blessed are the peacemakers," not, "Blessed are the peace lovers." Sometimes we have to be "troublesome peacemakers". Think of Gideon after he had met with *Yahweh Shalom*. For him the policy of appeasement and compromise came to an abrupt end; he had to risk his life. And taking on the Midianites was going to be dangerous in the extreme. The fact is that peace lovers, peace-at-any-price people, bear a measure of responsibility for the wrongdoing and injustice in the world. As we have seen, there is a better example than Gideon. The Prince of Peace himself was often at the centre of controversy. To do good is to oppose evil and to oppose evil is to court the disfavour of those perpetrating it.

Second, we can know his peace here and now. Not until Jesus is acknowledged as King of kings and Lord of lords will there be universal peace. But at a personal level we can know peace with God here and now. "Therefore, since we have been justified through faith, we have peace with God through our Lord Jesus Christ" (Rom. 5:1). The estrangement that came as a result of the fall has been decisively addressed. Our sin has been forgiven and our guilt taken away. What's more, "if, when we were God's enemies, we were reconciled to him through the death of his Son, how much more, having been reconciled, shall we be saved through his life? Not only is this so, but we rejoice in God through our Lord Jesus Christ, through whom we have now received reconciliation" (Rom. 5:10-11).

Third, there is also the sense of *shalom*--of well-being and serenity--that comes to our hearts and minds. The peace described in Scripture is primarily relational. It is a harmony between two or more parties. But by his presence in our lives, *Yahweh Shalom* also imparts a sense of peace. Paul encourages us to present our requests to God, with thanksgiving, and assures us that "the peace of God, which transcends understanding, will guard our hearts and minds in Christ Jesus" (Phil 4:7, 9). Sometimes it seems to descend as a gentle blanket. At other times it appears to emanate from within. God has already given us his Spirit: "The fruit of the Spirit is love, joy, peace. . ." (Gal. 5:22).

How wonderful that peace is! Yes, knowing and believing the truth can itself create a sense of peace. But there is more. The Spirit who indwells us creates fruit in our lives. One of the results of the presence of *Yahweh Shalom* is the experience of peace. At times the peace passes understanding. When our circumstances should naturally cause us anxiety or plunge us into turmoil, we experience the peace that only God can give.

Fourth, we are to be agents of God's peace in a world characterized by disharmony. An immediate by-product of our reconciliation with God is that he creates harmony between us and Christians of different backgrounds. There is a unique fellowship between the most unlikely of people (Eph 2:14-18). And God instructs us to be peaceable toward everybody. Jesus said, "Blessed are the peacemakers, for they will be called children of God" (Matt 5:9). Paul made it clear that there would be tension on account of the stand we take but he stressed that any hostility ought not to be on account of belligerence on our part: "If it is possible, as far as depends on you, live at peace with everyone" (Rom. 12:18; cf. I Pet.3:13-17; 4:12-16). As children of *Yahweh Shalom*, we ought in the here and now to provide a picture of the peace that will one day be universal.

Conclusion
For there to be genuine peace, it is necessary to address the root cause of the disharmony. God has done this in such a way as to make inner peace a present reality for those who receive his grace. Even in this as-yet-unredeemed-world, people can experience a measure of peace. To the extent that they bow to the lordship of Christ, they can experience peace. But it is a two-way street. Ultimately, when evil is vanquished, there will be universal peace. As those who have experienced the blessing of reconciliation with God and fellowship with our fellow-believers, we look forward to the day when all the causes of disharmony have been removed forever.

Right now, as children of God, we are to be peacemakers. But ironically, that could get us into trouble. Paul Insists: "Make it your ambition to lead a quiet life: You should mind your own business and work with your hands, just as we told you, so that your daily life may win the respect of outsiders and so that you will not be dependent on anybody" (1 Thess 4:11-12). As those who are committed to the ultimate cause, we ought not to get side-tracked into petty issues, but a stand for justice and truth may make us unpopular. Our motivation is not belligerence but peace. We may well pray the prayer attributed to St. Francis of Assisi:

> Lord, make me an instrument of your peace!
> Where there is hatred let me sow love;
> where there is injury, pardon; where there is doubt, faith;
> where there is despair, hope; where there is darkness, light;
> where there is sadness, joy.

Benediction

> The Lord bless you and keep you;
> the Lord make his face shine on you and be gracious to you;
> the Lord turn his face toward you and give you peace (Num 6:24-26).

> "Now may the Lord of peace himself give you peace at all times and in every way. The Lord be with you" (2 Thess 3:16).

יְהוָה צְבָאוֹת

Yahweh Ts'vaot: The LORD Almighty

Reading. Haggai 2:1-9

This morning we are looking at one of the great names of the Old Testament, probably you have missed it because you are reading the transliteration or the equivalent in English. It occurs 200 times in the Bible and used in a particular context. It is not a difficult one but there can be a bit of confusion.

In Haggai 2 you saw the repetition of the name Yahweh Ts'vaot or The LORD of Hosts in King James version or the LORD Almighty in the New International Version. The repetition might sound like redundancy. It is there for a reason.

When we read in the Old Testament The Lord Almighty or God Almighty, it is always a transliteration of Shaddai or El Shaddai. But when you read the LORD Almighty, it is Yahweh Ts'vaot.

Sooner or later we all find ourselves in situations that overwhelm us or are challenging. You are taken right out of your comfort zone and find that a set of circumstances has arisen which makes you ill at ease and facing an obstacle. Perhaps one thing comes on top of another or perhaps you face a situation that you have never faced before such as failing health, or selling your current home and moving. The ageing process brings its own challenges. It doesn't have to be very dramatic to make you feel that you are facing an overwhelming situation that you have never faced before. At such a time it is of huge importance to see God as he has revealed himself in the passages, we will look at today, as the LORD Almighty, Yahweh Ts'vaot.

SO, LET'S SEE EXACTLY WHAT THIS NAME MEANS.

The concept of Ts'vaot is quite simple. Ts'vah in Hebrew is an army or "a host" - . Ts'vaot is the plural. It means much more that God is LORD of the armies of Israel. The Bible tells us that at the end of a period of 430 years, to the very day, "all the LORD's hosts (Ts'vaot - צְבָאוֹת) left Egypt" (Ex 12:41).

The term is sometimes used to refer to the angels of God. So we read, for example, in Psalm. 103:20-21:
> Praise the LORD, you his angels,
> you mighty ones who do his bidding,
> who obey his word.
> Praise the LORD, all his heavenly hosts,
> you his servants who do his will.
> (Cf. Ps. 148:2)

I think it was F.B. Meyer (I can't trace the quote) that said,

"When we think of Yahweh Ts'vaot, we conceive of angels and worlds, (of the armies of heaven and the elements of matter), or winds and waves, of life and death as a vast ordered army obeying the commands of their captain, Yahweh Ts'vaot."

A VERY DEFINITE PICTURE IS BEGINNING TO EMERGE.

David
The word providence comes to mind, one of my favourite words, because it speaks of God's ability to control everything, to co-ordinate things to bring about his perfect purpose.

Now I think this becomes crystal clear as we look at a few well-known examples from Scripture. When you face an overwhelming situation, you need to be aware of the fact that Yahweh Ts'vaot is in the picture.

Think of the ts'vaot of Israel quivering in their boots as Goliath marches up and down insulting them and defying them. They were arch enemies of the Israel. They were advanced militarily, exceptionally well trained, lived near the Gaza strip of today and were the first to use metal tips on their spears. Here they are on Israel soil and threatening them. For 40 days Goliath invites the Israelites to a dual while issuing the challenge on Israel soil!

Israel's morale is incredibly low and it is at this point that David arrives on the scene on an errand for his father. He is delivering it when Goliath appears and starts his taunts. David's perspective is different from the Israelite army. He hadn't been there for 40 days to hear the insults but he had been in the wilderness communing with God looking after the sheep, seeing them as God's sheep, tackling a lion and a bear in the name of the Lord, exposing himself to danger and being victorious.

David can hardly believe that a man could be so audacious as to challenge the armies of the living God. At this stage David is likely an older teenager rather than a young boy and certainly old enough and big enough to try on Saul's armour and to be offered Saul's daughter. David does not believe that this Philistine can triumph. He first of all collects 5 smooth stones from the brook.

Eventually young David went out to meet him. Goliath was insulted when he saw that David was just a boy and that he had come out with a staff and a sling. "Am I a dog, that you come to me with sticks? And the Philistine cursed David by his gods..."

David's response goes right to the heart of the matter:
> "You come against me with a sword and spear and javelin, but I come against you in the name of Yahweh Ts'vaot, the God of the armies of Israel, who you have defied. This day the LORD will hand you over to me" (1 Sam 17:45-46).

We know the story of how David used his sling and the little stone penetrated the most vulnerable spot of Goliath's armour.

The point is that Yahweh Ts'vaot was in total charge. It was God who had created the law of gravity. It was he who created the atmosphere around and above us. It is he who established the laws of aerodynamics and the human body with its points of vulnerability. It was he who had looked upon David and the sheep in the wilderness and given him the ability to use the sling.

As Yahweh Ts'vaot he was able to marshal all these things to fulfil his purpose.

It looked like a mismatch but David had a different perspective. He didn't just see Goliath. He saw in the same picture, Goliath and God. Goliath the giant became a midget because David realised that the battle was not between him and the giant. The real battle was between Goliath and Yahweh Ts'vaot.

The truth of the matter that in everything we undertake God is either in the picture or he is not. When he is not, Goliaths look their size and we cringe and shrink in fear.

A number of years ago I was involved in a Franklin Graham campaign in Johannesburg, South Africa, we had an executive committee and we were working towards three nights in a huge soccer stadium. We had the committee meetings with the member of the Graham organisation and initially all the reports are edifying. But the final meeting before the stadium meetings, suddenly all sorts of things were going wrong – traffic reports, travel reports, weather reports, and other aspects were not finalised. Gloom descended on the meeting. This was a huge undertaking and there were so many loose ends and we were facing troubles. Then we came to a report by a man who worked for the Navigators and I wondered what negative news he would bring. He paused for a moment and said: "God is in big trouble." Everyone kept quiet for a second and then what he said sank in, we all burst out laughing because of our foolishness.

This was God's enterprise and he was in total control. Yes, we had our obstacles but it went off because God can never be in big trouble. We can but when he is in the picture, it makes all the difference.

So, when the situation seems overwhelming and God is in the picture, it changes the perspective entirely.

After a devastating disappointment, it is important to realise that God is Yahweh Ts'vaot.

Isaiah
King Uzziah had been a remarkably successful king, a godly king. His fame stretched far and wide and he ruled for a long time. Then the Bible tells us that God helped him wonderfully until he was successful and then pride led to his downfall. Uzziah intruded into the priest's office and did what no king was allowed to do – but he was king after all – and immediately God struck him with leprosy.

He had to live in a home away from everybody and had a vice-regent take care of his kingdom. He died a leper.

Isaiah had very easy access to the royal court. You can imagine the devastation in this young man's life as he may have pinned his hopes to a godly king and God's hand upon Israel when suddenly this tragic end to King Uzziah life. Isaiah was able to write:

> In the year that King Uzziah died, I saw the Lord seated on a throne, high and exalted, and the train of his robe filled the temple. Above him were the seraphim, each with six wings. With two wings they covered their faces, with two they covered their feet, and with two they were flying. And they were calling to one another,
>> Holy, holy, holy -
>> Is the LORD Almighty; (Yahweh, Ts'vaot)
>> The whole earth is full of his glory
>
> At the sound of their voices the doorposts and thresholds shook and the temple was filled with smoke.
> "Woe is me!" I cried. 'I am ruined! For I am a man of unclean lips, and I live among a people of unclean lips, and my eyes have seen the king, the LORD Almighty (Yahweh Ts'vaot)."
> (Isa 6:1-4).

The Lord commissions Isaiah.

It is a wonderful picture we are given and the point is quite simple. Encouragement comes when we realise who it is who is seated on the throne of the universe. So the psalmist says when the foundations are being destroyed, "What shall the righteous do?" He comes back immediately "Yahweh is in his holy temple. Yahweh is on his heavenly throne."

Disappointments may come but not as severe as that of Isaiah, but at times when they come upon us, it is always good to remember it is he who is Yahweh Ts'vaot, the Lord of the armies, the one is in control of everything, harmonises everything and brings about his desired end.

Haggai
A third example here is what happens when you face a really daunting task. The captives, God's people had returned from exile, they really did put first things first. Not only did they forego relative ease in Babylonia, they gave freewill offerings toward the rebuilding of the house of God on its site. They began to build at the first possible opportunity.

But, as a result of sustained opposition on the part of the surrounding people they downed tools and for 15 years in the face of huge opposition, not another stone was laid. Meanwhile they worked on their own homes. The opposition ceased but things just didn't work out for them.

God raised up two prophets, Haggai and Zechariah who challenged the people to recommence the building of the temple. The people heeded their message and got stuck in.

After a month God spoke to them again. My guess is that they may have been losing heart. The dating of the prophecy is important (Lev. 23:33; Hag. 2:1). The Feast of Tabernacles was a time when, among other things, the harvest was celebrated (Lev 23:39-43).

But, although they were obeying God, their harvest was meagre and there was so much to do. The foundations did not look so impressive. The opposition had not gone away. Imagine the situation of the people and the force this message must have come to them.

Now let's read this amazing passage with the meaning of the name Yahweh Ts'vaot in mind.

> On the twenty-first day of the seventh month, the word of the Lord came through the prophet Haggai: "Speak to Zerubbabel son of Shealtiel, governor of Judah, to Joshua son of Jozadak, the high priest, and to the remnant of the people. Ask them, 'Who of you is left who saw this house in its former glory? How does it look to you now? Does it not seem to you like nothing? But now be strong, Zerubbabel,' declares the Lord. 'Be strong, Joshua son of Jozadak, the high priest. Be strong, all you people of the land,' declares the LORD, 'and work. For I am with you,' declares **the LORD Almighty** (Yahweh Ts'vaot). 'This is what I covenanted with you when you came out of Egypt. And my Spirit remains among you. Do not fear.'
>
> "This is what **the LORD Almighty** (Yahweh Ts'vaot) says: 'In a little while I will once more shake the heavens and the earth, the sea and the dry land. I will shake all nations, and what is desired by all nations will come, and I will fill this house with glory,' says **the LORD Almighty** (Yahweh Ts'vaot). 'The silver is mine and the gold is mine,' declares **the LORD Almighty** (Yahweh Ts'vaot). 'The glory of this present house will be greater than the glory of the former house,' says **the LORD Almighty** (Yahweh Ts'vaot). 'And in this place I will grant peace,' declares **the LORD Almighty** (Yahweh Ts'vaot)" (Haggai 2:1-9).

What a message! The repetition is not by accident. It is Yahweh Ts'vaot, the one who owns everything and can co-ordinate everything.

Guess what happened? Things took a turn for the worse. The building inspector arrived in the person of Tattenai, the governor of the province of Trans-Euphrates. He wanted to know who had authorized the building operation and took down a list of the names of the men working on the construction. They were in big trouble or so it seemed. A report was sent to King Darius who ordered that a search be made in the archives at Babylon. There they found a copy of the decree of Cyrus. Accordingly Darius issued the following instructions to the provincial officials,

> Stay away from there. Do not interfere with the work on this temple of God … . The expenses of these men are to be fully paid out of the royal treasury … so that the work will not stop … Whatever is needed … must be given to them daily without fail … Furthermore, I decree that if anyone changes this edict, a beam is to be pulled from his own house and he is to be lifted up and impaled upon it … His house is to be made a pile of rubble. May God who has caused his Name to dwell there, overthrow any king or people who lifts a hand to change this decree or to destroy this temple in Jerusalem. I, Darius have decreed it. Let it be carried out with diligence.

They had to do what they could and God, Yahweh Ts'vaot, undertook to do what only he could. He is the one who marshals friends and foes to serve his purpose. He is the General in overall command.

We know the great dictum of Hudson Taylor, missionary pioneer said: "God's work, done in God's way, will never lack God's provision." This is not an incentive to reckless behaviour. We must use our common sense. We must be led by the Lord, of course, but it is quite amazing how God provides. We see it in scripture again and again. We have seen this work out in various circumstances. I could write a book of incredible stories of God's amazing provision.

I think of an American woman who was in Cape Town many years ago who saw some street urchins. Her heart was stirred and she asked one, "Can you tell me where you live?" This glue-sniffing child took her, in an up-market area, to the canal where there was a hole in the cement wall where he slept. Her heart was so moved that she felt something had to be done. She didn't have the where-with-all but she took one step after the other speaking to one here and there When I became Area Minister there was a home for these children. Money had come from all over the world and the first group were just passing through Grade 12.

In another circumstance a colleague of mine had a vision to build a Christian school. I went out with them and some others to view property. We stood and looked at some fields. I couldn't see it but they could. They could see a building, see a school where there was nothing. They didn't build on that site but the vision was there. Out of the blue there was a derelict school they didn't know about. They purchased the building; God provided the money. A cult had offered more than twice as much. The trust that owned the land decided to sell it to them to have a school operating on the site. Today it is a thriving school with wonderful staff, preschool up to Grade 12. It came from nowhere – God had provided and poured the money in.

We have heard from Susan and Frank Janetti, Zimbabwe Gecko Society, just recently of the most amazing provision that God has made in their ministry.

Conclusion

This is Yahweh Ts'vaot! The silver is his and the gold is his. There is no limit to what he can do. It is a matter of hearing and trusting him. He can do immeasurably more than we can ask or even imagine.

The bottom line is this: either we bring him into the picture or we don't. In every circumstance you either see it without God or with God.

In our committee meeting we were all momentarily seeing the obstacles but not seeing the presence of God. When it was said: "God is in big trouble now!" it brought sanity to the meeting. God is in total charge. It is never a question whether he is able. He is Yahweh Ts'vaot. It is only a question of whether it is his will.
We obviously don't want anything that is outside of his will. We don't have to suspect that he cannot accomplish that which he wants to accomplish. He is Yahweh Ts'vaot, the faithful God who commits himself to us and who marshals all events and resources to his glory.

Won't you place your trust in him afresh, in your circumstance right now.

Whatever we do, let's trust him!

יְהוָה רֹעִי

Yahweh Ro'i: The LORD is my Shepherd

Reading: Psalm 23

There are many wonderful psalms but this one is the best known and probably the best loved of them all.

It takes up a theme that recurs in many places in Scripture. But there are those who say that we should substitute something else to convey the same truths. Its imagery was familiar to those in the Middle-East but half of the world's population lives in cities and is unfamiliar with sheep and shepherding. So, they say, we should try to retain the thoughts but jettison the imagery.

It is a sincere but ill-considered suggestion. The motivation is to make the message relevant to 21st century city-dwellers.

But we can't do that. In interpreting the Bible we ask, "What did it mean to the original hearers in their situation and what then does it mean to us in our situation?" We cannot attempt to take a short cut here without doing a huge injustice to Scripture. We ought not to confuse the *text itself* and the *explanation* of the text.

Far too much is lost. There simply isn't a better picture. With relatively little effort we can appreciate the rich imagery and derive spiritual benefit from this great psalm.

NOT SURPRISINGLY, THE SHEPHERDING IMAGE IS ONE OF THE MOST PROMINENT IN SCRIPTURE (Both Old and New Testaments).

Yes, this is no doubt because **sheep and shepherds were a common sight in Israel.**

1. Both kings and spiritual leaders are depicted as shepherds.
2. In a crushing denunciation of the nation's spiritual leaders, God says, *"Woe to the shepherds of Israel who only take care of themselves. Should not shepherds take care of the flock?"* (Ezek 34:2).
3. You may remember that when Jesus saw the crowd who flocked to hear him, *"he had compassion on them because they were like sheep without a shepherd"* (Mark 6:34).
4. Jesus referred to himself as the Good Shepherd (John 10:1– 18).
5. Paul instructed the elders of the church in Ephesus to *"be shepherds of the church of God which he bought with his own blood"* (Acts 20:28).

The imagery is very appropriate indeed.

PSALM 23: AN EXTENDED ANALOGY.

We are going to walk through this great psalm with the help of a man called Phillip Keller.

Keller, who died in 1997, was a Canadian; in later life, he lived in British Columbia but he grew up in Kenya. In fact, some here knew Phillip Keller. He has a relative in the church. I mentioned him once before and Pastor Benny Jones of White Rock Baptist explained what a profound impact Keller had on his life. Probably the best known of his **35** books is a book entitled ***A Shepherd looks at Psalm 23.***[16]

---

[16] W Phillip Keller, (1920 – 1997), *A Shepherd Looks at Psalm 23,* Zondervan

I am <u>deeply indebted to him</u> for his insights. Much of what I am going to say is based on this best-selling classic. I will not keep saying, "According to Phillip Keller," but I wish to acknowledge his contribution upfront.

In the difficult years that followed the Great Depression, Keller, the son of missionary parents in Kenya, scraped together his hard-earned money and bought a small flock of 30 sheep. As a hands-on sheep farmer he developed a healthy and contented flock. His insights really help us to "get inside" this psalm.

Identifying with David

From what Keller says, he cared for his flock much as young David had cared for his father's sheep. You may recall that when King Saul asked young David what qualified him to go and fight with monstrous Goliath, he responded: *"Your servant has been keeping his father's sheep. When a lion or a bear came and carried off a sheep from the flock, I went after it, struck it and rescued the sheep from its mouth. When it turned on me, I seized it by its hair, struck it and killed it"* (1 Sam 17:34-35).

> Years later, when David became king, God said to him, *"You are to shepherd my people Israel and you will become their ruler"* (2 Sam 5:2).

In all likelihood, the psalm was written in the latter years of David's life when he was ruling as king in Jerusalem.

He looked back on his days as a shepherd and remembered his care for the flock in his charge. He had diligently and lovingly cared for the flock in his care. As he thought of God's loving provision and protection, he realised that **what he had done imperfectly, God does perfectly.**

Not fanciful (this is not quite an allegory, so we don't have to force the parallels and assign a meaning to everything mentioned; it is an extended analogy)

SO LET'S WALK THROUGH THIS GREAT PSALM (We'll gallop).

Three preliminary observations will help us
Sheep need a shepherd. Many animals are able to survive without human help. They know by instinct what they need to do to ward off animals of prey. They know where to find food. But not sheep!

Keller was a diligent and wise sheep farmer. He did what was necessary to provide pasture for his healthy flock. But his neighbour was a tenant sheep-man with a scrawny, emaciated, sickly flock. He neglected his land and many of his sheep died. Some fell prey to dogs and cougars and rustlers. They had only polluted, muddy water to drink. He comments in his book: "In my mind's eye, I can still see them standing at my fence, huddled sadly in little knots, staring wistfully through the wires at the rich pastures on the other side" (p. 29). The contrast helps us to appreciate good shepherding.

Keller argues, I think convincingly, that *the psalm starts during the winter months* at the ranch and proceeds to the highlands during the summer months.

"The LORD is my Shepherd; I lack nothing"
First there is a general statement: "The LORD is my Shepherd (*Yahweh Ro'i*); I lack nothing." I could be the only person who has had a problem with this line. As a child I was taught to recite this psalm in the King James Version. I could never quite understand why we could say the LORD's my shepherd and then negate the sentiment by saying that we did not want him.

He is all I could ever need. I suppose the word that sums it all up is the word **"contentment"**. Here is a happy sheep. But not all sheep are happy. This depends largely on the quality of the shepherd. **David knew what he did as a diligent shepherd**. But he knew that, with the best will in the world, he could not be everywhere and that sometimes a sheep would get itself into real trouble, go astray, fall down a cliff, fall over onto its back and be unable to get itself back onto its feet, pick up a parasite, and become sick. He understood his own shepherd's heart but he also knew his limitations. **Then he realised that there is a Shepherd who has no limitations, who knows the terrain completely, whose judgement is perfect, whose care is infinite, and whose competence is complete**. So he is able to approach the subject from the perspective of a satisfied sheep.

"He makes me lie down in green pastures"
I don't think we understand how important it is that sheep are able to lie down. But for a sheep to lie down, **four requirements** have to be met.

It has to be free from the fear of predators
Keller tells of an occasion when a visitor brought **a Pekingese puppy** along, opened the car door and that set 200 of his sheep rushing across the field in panic. Timid! *Nothing reassured his flock as to see him in the field.*

It has to be free from friction with other sheep
It surprised me to know that there is often tension and rivalry among the sheep. Just as there is a pecking order among chickens, there is a **"butting order"** among sheep. And a sheep has to stand up to defend its rights. *But often the sight of the shepherd puts an end to the fighting.*

It has to be free from flies and other pests
Sheep can **be driven to distraction by nasal flies, bot flies, warble flies and ticks**. They cannot lie down when they are tormented by these pests. They are up on their feet, stamping their legs, shaking their heads, ready to rush off into the bush for relief from the pests. *The shepherd has to take steps to protect the sheep from these pests.*

It has to be free from hunger
Green pastures are the product of hard labour. Besides the clearing of fields, grains and legumes need to be seeded and planted and irrigated. A hungry, ill-fed sheep is ever on its feet, searching for another scanty mouthful to try to satisfy its gnawing hunger.

We could obviously draw spiritual lessons out of all of these aspects. *But suffice it to say here that it is the presence of the shepherd that makes all the difference in each of them.*

"He leads me beside quiet waters"
Here again, the key to where clean water is to be found lies with the shepherd. **Dehydration** can have a devastating effect of sheep. They obtain some water from the morning dew. But if sheep are thirsty, they will search out water. They may find it in **polluted potholes and pick up internal parasites**. So the shepherd needs to know the whereabouts of wells and springs, and streams. He leads me beside quiet waters.

"He refreshes (restores) my soul"
At times a sheep will lose its footing and fall over onto its back. And it cannot get up. It is a pathetic sight; it flays away frantically. It may bleat a little but usually it lies there lashing about in frightened frustration. There is an old English term for a sheep in this predicament. They say it is **a "cast" sheep**. If the owner does not arrive on the scene in a very short time, the sheep will die. The gasses

tend to build up in the **rumen** or first stomach and cut off the blood circulation to the extremities of the body. This helps us to understand the urgency depicted in the Lord's parable of the shepherd who leaves the 99 sheep to go in search of the one. Keller tells us that he would often reach a sheep in the nick of time, place it on its wobbly legs and rub them to restore the circulation, talking to it gently as he rubbed those legs: **"I'm so glad I found you in time, you rascal."**

There are times when we get ourselves into trouble. He does not abandon us or shoot us. Even his rebuke is an expression of concern.

"He guides me along the right paths for his name sake".
Sheep are notorious creatures of habit. Unless led and prodded, they will follow the same trails until they become **ruts** and graze the same hills until they become **desert wastes**. "No other class of livestock requires more careful handling, more detailed direction, than do sheep" (p. 71). So a shepherd would need to ensure that there was **proper rotation**. They would need the flock to follow the right paths and be introduced to fresh pasture.

"Even though I walk through the darkest valley, I will fear no evil, for *you* are with me."
Summer is on its way. It is at this point that the shepherd is leading the sheep away from the home ranch towards the distant summer ranges. Here the companionship between sheep and shepherd is crucial. You notice the shift from **3rd person to 2nd person**.

Of course, **there is danger, more so than on the home ranch**. This is unfamiliar territory. There are rampaging rivers, rock slides, and predators. **The way to the summer plateau is by way of the darkest valley**, the valley of deep darkness, the "valley of the shadow of death." It can be scary but it is the best way to the uplands. If a sheep could think, it may want to argue with the shepherd. Why not take a more direct route, one that has more light? But the shepherd knows that this is the way to the summer grazing. **It may be dark, but it is negotiable**, and it contains water and food. There are dangers aplenty, but the shepherd is at hand.

"Your rod and staff, they comfort me"
So much could be said about the rod and the staff, but I shall confine myself to a few observations. The shepherd would carry a minimum of equipment. But always, he would have a rod and a staff. The staff was a long, narrow stick with a crook at the one end. The rod was shorter, and thicker and heavier at one end. Shepherds practiced using their rods, sometimes having competitions. They used them to **defend themselves and their flocks**. They also used them - sometimes throwing them to arrest a wayward sheep in its tracks. They were also used to examine the sheep's hide by parting the wool.

The staff was used to draw the sheep together, and sometimes to pull a sheep from harm's way or guide it when it is wandering away. At times a shepherd will use the crook in the staff to lift a newborn lamb to make sure that the mother will not reject her offspring because of the odour of human hands on it.

"You prepare a table before me in the presence of my enemies"
Remember, this is an extended analogy. Obviously sheep do not eat at a table. But the summer plateau with fresh pasture is like a table. And a shepherd would often undertake a **preparatory trip** to ensure that noxious weeds were removed and clearing debris from water holes. This preliminary inspection would help ensure the well-being of the flock.

Predators were never far away. Yet they could be kept at bay by the presence of the shepherd.

"You anoint my head with oil; my cup overflows"
But even on the summer ranges, *especially* on the summer ranges, insects are a nuisance. Summer time is fly time. Hoards of insects appear. The golden summer months can turn into a time of torture. The **nasal fly** can be particularly irritating. They buzz around the sheep's head and attempt to deposit their eggs in the damp mucous membranes of the sheep's nose. If they are successful, the eggs hatch causing irritation and inflammation. The sheep becomes frantic. But the shepherd would apply an oil-based mixture and this would help keep the flies at bay. It was also an antidote to the development of **a highly contagious scab** caused by a parasite. The psalmist concludes, "My cup runs over." The shepherd has made provision for every eventuality.

"Surely goodness and love will follow me all the days of my life and I will dwell in the house of the LORD forever"
Finally, the sheep sees no possibility of a change. He returns to the 3rd person. You may remember the psalm from the KJV, where is says "Goodness and *mercy*." Actually the word is *hesed*. It is translated in various ways. It combines the thought of **deep love and compassion with the thought of unerring permanence**. It is sometimes translated *"steadfast love"*. It is the love of God that endures forever.

THE GOOD SHEPHERD

I cannot leave this study without briefly but meaningfully considering the ultimate Good Shepherd.

In Ezekiel 34, the LORD strongly rebukes the self-serving shepherds of Israel. Then he gives a mind-blowing assurance. *"For this is what the Sovereign Lord says: I myself will search for my sheep and look after them. As shepherds look after their scattered flocks when they are with them, so will I look after my sheep . . . . I will place over them* *one shepherd, my servant David, and he will tend them; he will tend them and be their shepherd.* (Ezek 34:11-12, 22-23).

Now, can you see the significance of Jesus saying, "I am the Good Shepherd"? If the shepherd in Psalm 23 was crucial to the life of the sheep, how important is the ultimate Shepherd to us. *"I am the good shepherd. The good shepherd lays down his life for the sheep. . . . The reason my Father loves me is that I lay down my life—only to take it up again. No one takes it from me, but I lay it down of my own accord. I have authority to lay it down and authority to take it up again"* (John 10:1-18).

And, to complete the picture, we have Jesus' own assurance, *"My sheep listen to my voice; I know them, and they follow me. I give them eternal life, and they shall never perish; no one will snatch them out of my hand. My Father, who has given them to me, is greater than all; no one can snatch them out of my Father's hand. I and the Father are one"* (John 10:27-30).

Conclusion
Some years ago I read of an occasion when an actor was asked to recite the 23rd psalm at a gathering. His dramatic ability, his resonant voice, and his impeccable diction drew the admiration of those present. Someone in the crowd had heard an elderly country minister preach on the psalm, and the minister happened to be in attendance. He asked if the minister would also recite the psalm. The old vicar was reluctant to do so, but the people were insistent and so he obliged.

Something unusual happened. Untrained in speech and drama and with less-than-perfect enunciation, the old minister recited the psalm right from his heart. The people were deeply moved as the truth contained in each line struck home. Many tears were shed. One of the assembled guests expressed his amazement at the impact. Turning to the person next to him, he said, "I don't understand. What was the difference?" His neighbour replied, "Ah: the actor knows the 23rd psalm, but the minister knows the Shepherd!"

That is the most important distinction of all.

יְהוָה צִדְקֵנוּ

Yahweh Tsidqenu: The LORD our Righteousness

Readings: Jeremiah 23:5-6; Romans 10:1-4

If I were only allowed to preach on one of the names of God, I would probably choose this one: *Yahweh Tsidqenu*: the LORD Our Righteousness. I love them all. Each contributes to the overall picture. But this one brings us face to face with our greatest need—and God's greatest provision.

NOT TOO LONG AGO I HEARD SOMEONE SAY: "I REALLY DON'T LIKE THAT WORD, 'RIGHTEOUSNESS'".

That is problematic: It's one of the key terms in Scripture used in its noun and adjectival forms several hundred times. And the term "justify" means "to declare righteous."

I soon discovered what the difficulty was. (It is a difficulty you may have too). The person was thinking of *self*-righteousness. Someone who is pious and perhaps holier-than-thou; someone who possibly tries to score religious points and tends to be judgemental towards others, someone in whose company we lesser human beings feel decidedly awkward.

In some ways, this accords with a general view that there are good people and bad people in the world. Righteous people are good and will possibly reap the rewards of their good conduct (at least they are trying to be good); others have just got to hope for the best. Perhaps God will turn a blind eye to our sin. Or maybe he grades us on a curve and will take the top 50%. So it is really a matter of whether we are better than others.

Some here may labour under this misapprehension, possibly in a more refined form.

The good news is that this is not how things are. The Bible gives us a very different picture. You and I do not have to simply hope for the best.

God instituted a plan to ensure that every last one of us can be completely and winsomely righteous in his sight. In fact, this is one of the great themes of Scripture.

TO APPRECIATE THIS WE NEED TO FOLLOW A FASCINATING STREAM OF BIBLICAL PROPHECY.

The prophets **Isaiah, Jeremiah and Ezekiel** introduce us to a person called **"the Branch."** It seems like a strange title, doesn't it?

We first read about him in the early chapters of Isaiah:
> "A shoot will come up
> from the stump of Jesse (David's father),
> From his roots a Branch will bear fruit.
>
> The Spirit of the LORD will rest on him-
> the Spirit of wisdom and of understanding,
> the Spirit of counsel and of power,
> the Spirit of knowledge and of the fear of the LORD. . . .
> Righteousness will be his belt
> and faithfulness the sash around his waist (Isa 11:2-5).

Jeremiah takes up the same theme (our reading)
> "The days are coming,"

> declares the LORD,
> "when I will raise up to David
> a righteous Branch,
> a King who will reign wisely
> and do what is just and right in the land.
> In his days Judah will be saved
> and Israel will live in safety.
> This is the name by which he will be called:
> *Yahweh Tsidkenu*--the LORD our Righteousness" (Jer 23:5-6).

Again, Zechariah speaks of the one whose name is the Branch. He will be both a king and a priest (Zech 3 and 6).

How are we to understand this unusual designation? Actually, it's not all that difficult if we take things one step at a time.

Isaiah
You may recall the account in Isaiah 6 of the LORD's appearance to Isaiah: "In the year in which King Uzziah died I saw the Lord seated on a throne, high and exalted. . . ." (Isa 6:1-8). We know that Isaiah said, "Woe to me, I am ruined. . ." We know that the Lord asked him, "Whom shall I send and who will go for us?" and that Isaiah answered, "Here am I, send me." Usually that's where we leave the chapter.

But the rest of the passage is extremely significant. The Lord made it clear that Isaiah's ministry was not going to seem very successful. In fact, the people were going to disobey and their hearts would be calloused, rendering judgment inevitable. Isaiah's ministry, in other words, was to precipitate God's judgment (Isa 6:9-13). Then, when the cities lay in ruin and the people were in captivity, God would, in a sense, make a fresh beginning: "As the terebinth and oak leave stumps when they are cut down, so the holy seed will be the stump in the land" (Isa 6:13).

It is in this connection that Isaiah refers to one whom he describes as **"the Branch."**

Jeremiah adds the adjective "righteous." He is to be a king reigning on the throne of David. And he adds, "This is the name by which he will be called: *"Yahweh Tsidkenu*--the LORD our Righteousness."

THE CRUCIALLY-IMPORTANT SUBJECT OF RIGHTEOUSNESS COMES INTO SHARP FOCUS.

Righteousness is a comprehensive concept. It can be used to denote a person who is good, dependable and fair. The righteous are those who live life God's way. Often "the righteous" are contrasted with "the wicked" (Psa. 1:6; 37:16; Prov. 10:11; Jer. 12:1; Hab. 1:13; Mal. 3:18; Matt. 9:13; Rom. 5:7).

God is completely righteous
The Psalmist tells us: "The LORD is righteous in all his ways" (Psa 145:17); "Your righteousness is everlasting" (Psa. 119:142).

His standard is absolute. That is the thrust of Paul's argument in the first three chapters of Romans. He shows that Gentiles are accountable to God because they have chosen to suppress the light they have received through nature and conscience. Jews cannot feel superior because they have the Law. That, of course, is a great privilege (Rom. 3: 1-2), but it only serves to compound their guilt (Rom. 2:12-13). Listen to the way Paul summarizes:

> "We have already made the charge that Jews and Gentiles alike are under sin. Now we know that whatever the law says, it says

to those who are under the law, so that every mouth may be silenced and the whole world may be held accountable to God. Therefore no-one will be declared righteous in his sight by observing the law; rather, through the law we become conscious of sin (Rom. 3: 9, 19-20).

All this leads to his great announcement:

> "But now apart from the law the righteousness of God has been made known, to which the Law and the Prophets testify. This righteousness is given through faith in Jesus Christ to all who believe" (Rom 3:21)
>
> "If others think they have reasons to put confidence in the flesh, I have more: circumcised on the eighth day, of the people of Israel, of the tribe of Benjamin, a Hebrew of Hebrews; in regard to the law, a Pharisee; as for zeal, persecuting the church; as for righteousness based on the law, faultless.
>
> But whatever were gains to me I now consider loss for the sake of Christ. What is more, I consider everything a loss because of the surpassing worth of knowing Christ Jesus my Lord, for whose sake I have lost all things. I consider them garbage, that I may gain Christ and be found in him, not having a righteousness of my own that comes from the law, but that which is through faith in Christ—the righteousness that comes from God on the basis of faith" (Phil 3:4-9).

Later he mourned that his unbelieving compatriots had missed the point altogether: "Since they did not know the righteousness that comes from God and sought to establish their own, they did not submit to God's righteousness. Christ is the end of the law so that there may be righteousness for everyone who believes" (Rom 10:3-4).

The Basis of this Righteousness
Paul explains the basis of this righteousness: *"God made him who had no sin to be sin for us, so that in him we might become the righteousness of God"* (2 Cor. 5:21). **Here is what was happening on the cross. God looked upon his Son and said, "The wages of sin is death. You must die!" so he could look at you and me and say, "The gift of God is eternal life. You may live!"** *"Christ also suffered once for sins, the righteous for the unrighteous, to bring you to God"* (1 Pet 3:18).

Conclusion
Each of these titles of God emphasizes an important truth about God's nature. But this one probably tells us more of what we really *need* to know that any of the others, because it places the accent on what God has done for us in Christ. It conveys the lengths to which God has gone to procure your salvation and mine. He is *Yahweh Tsidqenu*--the LORD Our Righteousness. He is himself completely righteous, but the designation given to the Branch, the Son of David, is "The LORD *our* Righteousness." For that to be possible he had to come and live among us, and die for us. When we say, "*Yahweh Tsidqenu*" we are, in fact, declaring the gospel in just two words.

It is good news (not easy-believism). You need to trust him.

יְהוָה מְקַדִּשְׁכֶם

Yahweh Meqaddishchem: The LORD Who Makes You Holy

Readings: Leviticus 22:31-33; 1 Peter 1:13-25

There are people in all faiths who strive for lives of purity. In some cases, they are attempting to escape the contamination caused by sin. However they describe it, they are aware that there is something in the human situation that pollutes us. They want to escape it or to eliminate it or to overcome it.

Some have adopted extreme measures. They have tried to achieve holiness through self-denial and asceticism. Before he discovered the wonder of God's grace, Martin Luther believed that he had to mortify his propensity to sin by denying natural desires. He denied himself food and warmth, shivering in his cold cell. In his own words, he said: "I was a good monk and I kept the rule of my order so strictly that I may say that if ever a monk got to heaven by his monkery, it was I." The third century Alexandrian church father, Origen, is said to have castrated himself in the pursuit of holiness.

Others have opted for isolation, believing that if they removed themselves from the unhelpful influence of society, they could live lives of genuine holiness. But many of the hermits, who have gone into seclusion, and monks or nuns, who have cloistered themselves with like-minded people have discovered that they could not cloister themselves from themselves.

We have to take this matter seriously. Remember *"without holiness no one will see the Lord"* (Heb 12:14). Holiness is not presented to us in Scripture as an option, a nice-to-have.

So WHAT *IS* HOLINESS? And how do we come by it? Is it attainable in this life? Misconceptions abound. I like the way Kenneth Prior in his book *The Way to* Holiness identified a widespread caricature:

> For many people, the word, if it conveys anything at all, revives memories of stained-glass windows depicting pale and unhealthy-looking faces with bones clearly visible under a thin layer of flesh. . . . Always present, of course, is the inevitable halo to underline the utter impracticability of the whole idea.

Do you think of holiness like that? Many people do! As far as they are concerned, holy people are detached and hard to relate to, so heavenly minded that they are of no earthly use. You may admire them or you may correct the caricature as Kenneth Prior describes them:

> The holy men of the Bible are miles removed from such popular misconceptions. Instead of their being weak and anaemic, we find they are often tough with sun-burnt faces, like Elijah, John the Baptist and, be it reverently suggested, our Lord himself. . . Holiness, when rightly understood, is an attractive quality, not something forbidding and inhuman. [James Philip rightly observes:] "The greatest saints of God have been characterised, not by haloes and an atmosphere of distant unapproachability [sic], but by their humanity. They have been intensely human and lovable people with a twinkle in their eyes."

SO LET'S MAKE SURE WE ARE TALKING ABOUT THE BIBLICAL CONCEPT OF HOLINESS. WHAT EXACTLY IS HOLINESS?

We can equate the term 'holiness' with the term 'sanctification'. These English words translate the same Hebrew and Greek words. Similarly the verbs "sanctify" and "make holy" are equivalent.

The way to understand the meaning of any word is to examine the contexts in which it is used.

In the first place the word means "set-apart-ness." If something or someone is holy or sanctified, it is set apart from the ordinary or mundane. That which is sanctified is dedicated for a specific purpose. So a place could be holy, garments could be holy, utensils could be holy, and people could be holy.

But clearly, there is more to holiness than set-apart-ness.

As we study its usage, we see that there is an important moral dimension to holiness. Those who are holy do not conform to evil inclinations, they do what is good, they are self-disciplined and they resist evil desires and seek to be available to God (Titus 1:8; 1 Pet 1:13-16).

God is said to be holy; he is the ultimate in holiness. When Isaiah saw the Lord, he heard the seraphim calling out, "Holy, holy, holy. . . ." (Isa. 6:1-7). He never forgot that vision. For him God is "the Holy One of Israel" (Isa. 30:11, 12, 15; 40:25; 43:3, 14-15; 57:15). The psalmist declares, "You are enthroned as the Holy One" (Psa 22:3). In Revelation, we hear a great song, "Great and marvellous are your deeds Lord God Almighty. Just and true are your ways, King of the ages. Who will not fear you, O Lord, and bring glory to your name? For you alone are holy. All nations will come and worship before you, for your righteous acts have been revealed" (Rev 15:3-4).

God's holiness is indescribably glorious. It is associated with magnificent purity and splendour. The Psalmist encourages us to "worship the LORD in the beauty (splendour) of holiness" (Psa. 96:9). God is said to be "majestic in holiness (and) awesome in glory" (Ex 15:11). When we are given a picture of the throne of God that conveys reality, we see resplendent heavenly beings worshipping him. "Day and night they never stop saying, 'Holy, holy, holy is the Lord Almighty, who was, and is, and is to come'" (Rev. 4:8). When we loose sight of the holiness of God we fall short in our worship. Reverence is one of the first principles of worship because it is God we are worshipping.

Holiness in us is an attractive quality. It is not merely a sterile and dull absence of sin but the vibrant and glorious presence of goodness. There can be no element of self-righteousness (which is ugly) in true holiness. In the final analysis, to be holy is to be Christlike to be like Jesus.

THE MOST IMPORTANT THING WE CAN SAY ABOUT HOLINESS IS THIS: "ONLY GOD CAN MAKE US HOLY." This is the meaning of this name. *Yahweh Meqaddishchem* 'I am the Lord who makes you holy.'

We can say, "Without holiness no one will see the Lord; we can also say, "Without the Lord no one will see holiness."

We can take one of essentially three approaches:

Position 1: We could not save ourselves. God did his part in saving us by grace. Now, in gratitude, we have to do our part by living holy lives. So we should strive to be holy in response to God's goodness. *It's all up to us*.

Position 2: No more than we could save ourselves by our own righteousness can we sanctify ourselves by attempting to live holy lives. Anything we try to do will get in the way. ***It's all up to God***.

Position 3: Only God can make us holy, but we have an important role to play in the process. ***It's up to both God and us.*** Without his working, we *cannot* be holy; without our cooperation with him, we *will not* be holy!

All I shall say at this stage is that when we consider all the references a **beautiful, balanced picture** emerges.

The emphasis is on the positive, not the negative. In other words, holiness must be understood in terms of what we are rather than what we are not. If we think of holiness only as avoiding sin, we are missing the point altogether.

Sanctification or holiness is what God does in us as we are exposed to the work of the Holy Spirit within us. That leads us to the second most important thing we can say about holiness.

SANCTIFICATION (HOLINESS) IS A PROCESS THAT COMMENCES WHEN WE PLACE OUR TRUST IN THE LORD AND CONTINUES THOUGHOUT OUR LIVES.

Nowadays I am the proud owner of a digital camera, but not too long ago I was using my trusty old camera. I was attached to it and London Drugs did a roaring trade developing and printing my pictures. One of my granddaughters, who has only experienced digital cameras, was intrigued by this old-fashioned technology. She was surprised that she could not see the photograph in the monitor--immediately. Indeed, there was no monitor. Before the advent of digital technology, cameras worked on a simple principle. Inside the camera was a small chamber in which there was no light whatsoever. You inserted a roll of light-sensitive film which was stretched across the back of the dark chamber. When you took a photograph, you heard a clicking sound; it was the sound of a mechanism that opened the shutter for a fraction of a second allowing light to pass into the camera though the lens. The light took the form of an image and, in a moment, the image made an impression on the film. You had "captured" the scene.

But you did not yet have a picture. The film was later removed and developed in a dark-room. It was exposed to light and chemicals under controlled conditions. Slowly but surely the image began to appear. If you had been able to watch this development in the dark-room, you would have seen the image sharpen until the picture was a clear representation of the image created in the film by the light that passed through the aperture.

Jesus insisted that we must be born again for a very good reason. The rebirth involves a change of heart, a change wrought in us by God, himself. It's as though the light comes into our lives and makes an indelible impression. **Regeneration** or being born again has been described as the "act of God whereby the governing disposition of the soul is made holy." But that is only the beginning of the process. By exposure to the right conditions the image is developed. **Sanctification** further develops the image instilled in the flash of regeneration. It has been defined as the "continuous process whereby the holy disposition imparted in regeneration is maintained and strengthened." Through the ongoing work of the Holy Spirit, God transforms us into the likeness of his Son (Rom. 8:28-30; 2 Cor. 3:18).

What is absolutely essential to the process is the activity of the Holy Spirit within us. There is no neat formula, no magical moment, which places us in the "entirely sanctified" category.

Not simply passive recipients ("on" instead of "in")
Sanctification is the work of the Spirit in us, but we are not simply passive recipients of God's sanctifying activity, being worked 'on' rather than 'in.' We can and should do certain things to advance the process. It really does not help to try to distinguish between the part God plays in our sanctification and the part we play. Scripture does not allow for such a neat distinction and if we try to invent one, we shall probably take ourselves back into legalistic bondage.

God's work and our cooperative response are so closely related as to be, to all intents and purposes, indistinguishable. Paul's prayer for the Thessalonians is that "God himself, the God of peace, will sanctify you through and through and that your whole spirit, soul and body will be kept blameless at the coming of our Lord Jesus Christ." He immediately adds, "The one who calls you is faithful and he will do it" (1 Thess. 5:23-24). But that great benediction is preceded by a list of practical instructions, the last of which is, "Avoid every kind of evil." Paul urges the Philippians: "Continue to work out your salvation with fear and trembling for it is God who works in you to will and to act according to his good pleasure" (Phil. 2:12-13). Perhaps the clearest expression of the cooperative nature of the process is found in Paul's statement to the Colossians, "To this end I labour, struggling with all **his** energy, which so powerfully works in me" (Col. 1:29; emphasis added). If you struggling to grow in grace, it is not about being a better person, it is co-operating with God so that he my create in a picture of Jesus.

SO, WHAT CAN WE DO TO ADVANCE THE PROCESS?

Positive Approach

From a practical point of view, a positive approach achieves far more than a negative one. There are certain things we know we should not do. It is within our power to avoid them and we should certainly do so. We know they will not help us in our walk with the Lord. The question to ask is if it will help us in our walk with the Lord. Paul asks in 1 Corinthians 10:23 if it is beneficial.

But if this is all we do (or don't do) the emphasis is negative and we may become legalistic and joyless or even self-righteous. **Simply avoiding certain practices does not constitute sanctification.** It is almost certain to result in abject failure and defeat. If we try in our own strength to "battle our giants" or to overcome deep-seated habits or attitudes, this often leads to the kind of stalemate described in Romans 7:14-24. "I do not understand what I do. For what I want to do I do not do, but what I hate I do. . . . I have the desire to do what is good, but I cannot carry it out. For I do not do the good I want to do, but the evil I do not want to do—this I keep on doing" (Rom 7:15, 18, 19).

This is the key: living by the Spirit

That is why Paul lays such emphasis on "living by the Spirit" (Gal. 5:16). He describes what the Holy Spirit does in us: "The fruit of the Spirit is love, joy peace, patience, kindness, goodness, faithfulness, gentleness, and self-control." Most significantly he adds, "Against such things there is no law" (Gal. 5:22-23). If the focus is on the Spirit's control, and not the letter of the law, we fulfil the spirit of the law. The emphasis is on what we are, rather than what we do!

It's not that the commandments fall away. James, for example, makes it clear that there is a "royal law found in Scripture" (Jas. 2:8), and John tells us that if we say we know the Lord and don't keep his commandments, we are liars (1 John 2:4). Paul instructs us to "avoid every kind of evil" (1 Thess. 5:22). It's a question of how this is achieved. Think of some of the Ten Commandments: "Do not murder," "Do not steal," "Do not bear false testimony," and "Do not covet. . . ." (Ex. 20:13-17). "The fruit of the Spirit is love. . . ." That means that as the Holy Spirit influences me from within, the fruit of love grows in my life. How can I steal from one whom I love and how can I covet their possessions?

As simple as it may sound, we grow most not by intentionally avoiding sin but by exposing ourselves to God's activity through various "means of grace." Everything that will build us up, feed us spiritually, influence our thinking, and transform our attitudes will help the process of growth. Some of the negatives will drop out of our lives without our even realising it. We will change as the process of transformation continues. No haloes will appear around our heads but the beauty of Jesus will be seen in us. **Put simply, if we do what we can do, God will do what we can't do.** Or better, he will enable us to do what we can't do.

This wonderful teaching, which is developed in the New Testament, is present in the Old. It is such an integral part of God's nature as Yahweh, our covenant LORD, that he even incorporates his sanctifying activity into his name: "Consecrate yourselves and be holy, because I am the LORD, your God. Keep my decrees and follow them. . . . I am *Yahweh Mekaddishchem*--the LORD who sanctifies you" (Lev 20:7).

The process is described in 2 Corinthians 3. There is no time to explain this passage in detail, but listen to how Paul concludes this great passage: "*And we all, who with unveiled faces contemplate the Lord's glory, are being transformed into his image with ever-*

increasing glory, which comes from the Lord, who is the Spirit" (2 Cor 3:18).

Conclusion
God has always been "*Yahweh Mekaddishchem*—the LORD who sanctifies you." But his sanctifying work is especially evident under the New Covenant. The indwelling Spirit within us transforms us: "We, who with unveiled faces all reflect the Lord's glory, are being transformed into his likeness with ever-increasing glory, which comes from the Lord, who is the Spirit" (2 Cor. 3:18).

The question to ask is how serious am I that people see Jesus in me.

> Let the beauty of Jesus be seen in me,
> all his wondrous passion and purity.
> O Thou Spirit divine,
> all my nature refine,
> till the beauty of Jesus
> is seen in me.

Amen.

יְהוָה שָׁמָּה

Yahweh Shammah: The LORD is There

Reading. Ezekiel 43:1-6; 48:35

Now that Ascension day is no longer a public holiday (in Canada), we tend to forget Whit Sunday and the Day of Pentecost. In churches that follow the Christian calendar, attention is drawn to the fact that ten days after Jesus ascended, his promise regarding the Holy Spirit was fulfilled.

I shall never forget my first Whit Sunday service as a committed Christian. Appropriately, the focus of the service was on the coming of the Holy Spirit. During a time of open worship the church grew very quiet as we became aware of the Lord's presence. And then a dove came and perched on the windowsill and began to coo. As you know, the Spirit descended upon Jesus at his baptism in the form of a dove. This was just an ordinary dove whose timing was spot on. I would not be dogmatic but I think the Lord sent that bird to visit us as a reminder that his Spirit is among us. The extraordinary sense of his presence that we experienced, coupled with the gentle reminder from our little visitor left us in no doubt.

It so happens, this morning, that I am speaking on the name of God that is used to describe the Lord's presence among us. It is the name Yahweh Shammah. The subject we are about to consider is, I believe, a thrilling one. In fact, there can hardly be a more fitting way to conclude this study of the names of God than with a consideration of God as the one who is present with his people.

THERE CAN BE NO DOUBT WHATSOEVER THAT GOD IS EVERYWHERE.

One of the first things we are told about God is that he is omnipresent.

The Psalmist celebrates this reality in Psalm 139:

> Where can I go from your Spirit?
> Where can I flee from your presence?
> If I go to the heavens, you are there;
> if I make my bed in the depths, you are there.
> If I rise on the wings of the dawn,
> if I settle on the far side of the sea,
> even there your hand will guide me,
> your right hand will hold me fast.
>
> If I say, "Surely the darkness will hide me and the light become night around me,"
> even the darkness will not be dark to you;
> the night will shine like the day,
> for darkness is as light to you. (Ps. 139:7-12)

I love the way the philosopher, Empedocles expresses the thought:

> The nature of God is a circle of which the centre is everywhere and the circumference is nowhere.

So, God is everywhere.

BUT IT IS ALSO TRUE THAT HE CHOOSES TO MANIFEST HIS PRESENCE AT PARTICULAR TIMES AND PLACES.

One thinks of young Jacob who leaves home for the first time and sets out for the land of Haran. Imagine his churned up emotions as he leaves his parental home at Beersheba. He travels a day's journey, stops for the night and settles down to sleep with a stone for his pillow. In a dream, he sees a stairway that reaches from earth to heaven. Angels are ascending and descending on this stairway. Above it stands the LORD himself who reassures him regarding his protection and his promise.

> When Jacob awoke from his sleep, he thought, Surely the LORD is in this place, and I was not aware of it." He was afraid and said, "How awesome is this place! This is none other than the house of God; this is the gate of heaven." .... He called the place Bethel...(Gen. 28:16-17, 19).

You will remember that God gave very specific instructions regarding the construction of the tabernacle. It was to be made according to the exact pattern prescribed by him.

It was to be erected right in the centre of the encampment of Israel. It was to consist of an outer courtyard or enclosure and a sanctuary comprising a holy place and a holy of holies. There, in the heart of the sanctuary, at the centre of the whole structure, the ark of the covenant was to be placed.

It was a wooden chest containing the tablets of the law, a pot of manna and Aaron's rod that budded. It was overlaid with gold. On top of it was an atonement cover made of pure gold on which there were two statuettes of cherubim facing inwards.

Listen to what the Lord says:

> There, above the cover between the two cherubim that are over the ark of the Testimony, I will meet with you and give you all my commands for the Israelites.(Ex. 25:22).

When the tabernacle was completed ...

> When the cloud covered the Tent of Meeting, and the glory of the LORD filled the tabernacle. Moses could not enter the Tent of Meeting because the cloud had settled upon it, and the glory of the LORD filled the tabernacle. (Ex. 40:34-35).

The same was true of the temple. In his prayer King Solomon marvelled that God would deign to live among his people:

> But will God really dwell on earth? The heavens, even the highest heaven, cannot contain you. How much less this temple I have built! (1 Kgs 8:27).

But listen to what happened:

> When Solomon finished praying, fire came down from heaven and consumed the burnt offering and the sacrifices, and the glory of the LORD filled the temple. The priests could not enter the temple of the LORD because the glory of the LORD filled it. When all the Israelites saw the fire coming down and the glory of the LORD above the temple, they knelt on the pavement with their faces to the ground, and they worshipped and gave thanks to the LORD, saying, "He is good; his love endures for ever." (2 Chron. 7:1-3).

What was it that Elijah experienced in the cave at Mount Horeb?

The LORD said, "Go out and stand on the mountain in the presence of the LORD, for the Lord is about to pass by."

> Then a great and powerful wind tore the mountains apart and shattered the rocks before the LORD, but the LORD was not in the wind. After the wind there was an earthquake, but the LORD was not in the earthquake. After the earthquake came a fire but the LORD was not in the fire. And after the fire came a gentle whisper (the sound of a gentle quietness). When Elijah heard it, he pulled his cloak over his face and went out and stood at the mouth of the cave. (1 Kgs 19:11-13).

He knew the difference between a display of nature's force and the presence of the LORD.

So, this is the picture that emerges: God is present everywhere but, at certain times, he chooses to manifest his presence in special ways at particular places.

THE PROPHETS LOOK FORWARD TO A TIME WHEN GOD WILL BE PRESENT WITH HIS PEOPLE FOR EVER.

This theme is found, for example, in Isaiah and repeated by prophets like Jeremiah, Joel and Zechariah (Isa. 65:17-25; Jer. 31:31-34; Joel 3:17; Zech. 2:5; 14:8-9).

I would like to focus, this morning, on the prophet Ezekiel. His was an extremely difficult task. He and some of his compatriots had been taken into exile in Babylonia. But his fellow exiles were quite convinced that they would soon be back in Israel. For one thing, the temple was still standing and they were convinced that, because it was God's house, it was impregnable. After all his glory dwelt there.

Moreover, some false prophets were assuring them that their exile would be of short duration.

Ezekiel had to disabuse them. They were so hard of hearing that God instructed him to get up to all kinds of antics in order to get the message across. And God gave him special visions which formed the basis of his message. I find the vision in chapter ten particularly significant:

> The glory of the LORD rose from above the cherubim and moved to the threshold of the temple. The cloud filled the temple and the court was full of the radiance of the glory of the LORD.
>
> Then the glory of the LORD departed from over the threshold of the temple and stopped above the cherubim... They stopped at the entrance to the east gate of the LORD'S house, and the glory of the LORD of Israel was above them.
>
> The glory of the LORD went up from within the city and stopped above the mountain from the east of it.
>
> I told the exiles everything the LORD had shown me. (Ezek. 10:4, 18; 11:23, 25).

Toward the end of the book, Ezekiel is given a picture of the restoration of the city and the temple, a picture that looks way beyond an intermediate fulfilment.

> I saw the glory of the God of Israel coming from the east. His voice was like the roar of rushing waters, and the land was radiant with his glory. The vision I saw was like the vision I had seen when he came to destroy the city... and I fell face down.

> The glory of the LORD entered the temple through the gate facing east. Then the Spirit lifted me up and brought me into the inner court and the glory of the LORD filled the temple. ... I heard someone speaking to me from inside the temple. He said, "Son of man, this is the place of my throne and the place for the soles of my feet. This is where I will live among the Israelites for ever." (Ezek. 43:2-5)
>
> And the name of the city from that time on will be:
> THE LORD IS THERE (Ezek. 48:35).

We hear the same message in Revelation, only in a different way. As was appropriate given the circumstances, Ezekiel described the future in terms of a huge city and a great temple. Living water flowed from under the threshold of the temple not only supporting vegetation but even giving life to the Dead Sea.

In the Revelation the same truth is conveyed in a way more appropriate to the subsequent revelation God has given us:

> And I heard a loud voice from the throne saying, "Now the dwelling of God is with men, and he will live with them. They will be his people, and God himself will be with them and be their God."
>
> I did not see a temple in the city, because the Lord God Almighty and the Lamb are its temple. The city does not need the sun or moon to shine on it, for the glory of God gives it light and the Lamb is its lamp. (Rev. 21:3, 22-23)
>
> The throne of God and of the Lamb will be in the city, and his servants will serve him. They will see his face and his name will be on their foreheads. There will be no more night.(Rev. 22:3-4)

Well might we look forward to that great day.

BUT WAIT, THERE IS A PLACE WHERE GOD MANIFESTS HIS PRESENCE TODAY.

George Eldon Ladd has written a book entitled, *The Presence of the Future*. In it he shows that in a very real sense the future kingdom is present now.

One day we will live in a city called Yahweh Shammah. But, right here and now, God loves to meet with us.

In the New Jerusalem there will be no temple, no physical structure. The temple was a temporary measure. God himself will be there.

Now, we have only to read our New Testaments to see that we are described as the temple of the Holy Spirit.

That's what Paul says to the Corinthians:
> Don't you know that you yourselves are God's temple and that God's Spirit lives in you? (1 Cor. 3:16)
>
> We are the temple of the living God. As God has said, "I will live in them and walk among them, and I will be their God, and they will be my people." (2 Cor. 6:16).

He's even more explicit when he writes to the Ephesians:

> In him the whole building rises to become a holy temple in the Lord. And in him you too are being built together to become a dwelling in which God lives by his Spirit. (Eph. 2:21-22)

Since the Day of Pentecost, the experience of the Lord's presence should not be the exception but the norm. God wants to meet with us. We are his temple. He wants to manifest his glory among us. Whenever we come to him in sincere worship, he will make his presence felt. It will not always be the same. He is God. But we will know we have been in his presence.

Conclusion

Whenever we meet in Jesus' name, he is here, not just in the sense that he is omnipresent. We do not come just to reflect on his truth, nor even to commemorate his deeds. We come to meet with him. And, strange as it may seem to us, the LORD, Yahweh Shammah, really wants to meet with us. We are only just beginning to experience what it is like to enjoy his presence.

www.ingramcontent.com/pod-product-compliance
Lightning Source LLC
LaVergne TN
LVHW051237080426
835513LV00016B/1646